Advance Praise for *The Power of Reputation*

"*The Power of Reputation* is the definitive book on reputation and your career. Everyone who wants to build a career must read it. This powerful guide gives you the tools for success to make the most of your talents and, more important, to prepare you for when things don't go as planned. And, at some point in your career, you will be put to the test. There is no doubt of that. As Chris Komisarjevsky makes clear, reputation means everything, especially when the going is as tough as can be."

—*Tom Von Essen, New York City's 30th Fire Commissioner, during September 11, 2001; author of* Strong of Heart

"Chris Komisarjevsky has written a profound and practical book examining and illustrating the power and importance of one's reputation in determining the likelihood of success in the world of business and in all aspects of life. I encourage anyone seeking a better understanding of the roles that character, integrity, communication, ethics, and trust play in determining one's ability to impact others in positive and innovative ways to read this book carefully. Building on a vast store of practical knowledge and experience in the communications and public relations industry, Komisarjevsky employs a captivating style that makes it perfectly clear why reputation is anyone's most treasured asset—an asset that can take years or even a lifetime to build, but one that can be tarnished and destroyed in an instant as a result of an unethical decision or an immoral act. The reader will come away from this book with a clearer understanding of why character, communications, and trust are all integral to the process by which personal integrity and character are built. This book is a very valuable addition to the general business literature. Students, scholars, business executives, and the general public will find a wealth of practical advice on what is required to build and preserve a reputation undergirded by the integrity and trust that characterize enlightened ethical leadership."

—*William C. (Curt) Hunter, Dean of the Henry B. Tippie College of Business, University of Iowa*

"Given the growing impact of social media and personal branding on our lives and careers, *The Power of Reputation* couldn't have arrived at a better time. Chris Komisarjevsky successfully applies his vast experience in corporate reputation management to individual reputation, and shows us that the two actually have much in common."

—*Ron Alsop, author of* The 18 Immutable Laws of Corporate Reputation *and* The Trophy Kids Grow Up

"Like a good reputation, Chris Komisarjevsky's *The Power of Reputation* will stand the test of time. This is the ultimate testament to the author and his book. From understanding the foundation of good communication to implementing career strategies for achieving personal and professional goals in today's complex business and media environment, *The Power of Reputation* demonstrates how your reputation is the key to your success. Komisarjevsky provides the perfect combination of thoughtful personal insight, interesting examples, advice from business leaders, and the specific steps needed so the reader can negotiate the dangerous shoals that can destroy even the most highly cultivated reputation. In an age that glorifies ephemeral celebrity, the author has written a book of substance and character that explains the importance of reputation."

—Tobe Berkovitz, Ph.D., Associate Professor,
Boston University, College of Communication

"There are too many people nowadays writing books about subjects they have only thought about. Chris Komisarjevsky isn't one of them. Chris Komisarjevsky has actively managed the reputations of many corporations during his long career as the head of public relations firms. *The Power of Reputation* will make you understand how important your good name is. And you'll learn how to protect your reputation."

—John Crudele, Financial Columnist, New York Post

"In these times and in every career, reputation is king. Chris Komisarjevsky has done a masterful job in not only describing reputation's impact, but also how to manage one's reputation. This book is essential reading for anyone who cares about their reputation. And that's virtually everyone."

—Kevin Goldman, former Wall Street Journal *media reporter*
and author of Conflicting Accounts: The Creation and Crash
of the Saatchi & Saatchi Advertising Empire

The Power of Reputation

Strengthen the Asset That Will Make or Break Your Career

chris komisarjevsky

AMACOM AMERICAN MANAGEMENT ASSOCIATION
New York · Atlanta · Brussels · Chicago · Mexico City
San Francisco · Shanghai · Tokyo · Toronto · Washington, D.C.

Bulk discounts available. For details visit:
www.amacombooks.org/go/specialsales
Or contact special sales:
Phone: 800-250-5308
E-mail: specialsls@amanet.org
View all the AMACOM titles at: www.amacombooks.org

This publication is designed to provide accurate and authoritative information in regard to the subject matter covered. It is sold with the understanding that the publisher is not engaged in rendering legal, accounting, or other professional service. If legal advice or other expert assistance is required, the services of a competent professional person should be sought.

Library of Congress Cataloging-in-Publication Data

Komisarjevsky, Chris.
  The power of reputation : strengthen the asset that will make or break your career / Chris Komisarjevsky.
     p. cm.
Includes bibliographical references and index.
ISBN-13: 978-0-8144-1797-3
ISBN-10: 0-8144-1797-3
  1. Career development. 2. Reputation. 3. Business ethics. I. Title.
HF5381.K625 2012
650.1'3—dc23

2011045513

About AMA
American Management Association (www.amanet.org) is a world leader in talent development, advancing the skills of individuals to drive business success. Our mission is to support the goals of individuals and organizations through a complete range of products and services, including classroom and virtual seminars, webcasts, webinars, podcasts, conferences, corporate and government solutions, business books, and research. AMA's approach to improving performance combines experiential learning—learning through doing—with opportunities for ongoing professional growth at every step of one's career journey.

Printing number
10 9 8 7 6 5 4 3 2 1

To my family...

And to all those who believe
that reputation is to be treasured

contents

foreword

Even though we are a *Fortune 500* company, at Ryder we still strive to be like the hometown shopkeeper whose success is defined by the fact that your word and your good name mean everything. Our future depends on our reputation for trust and keeping promises. We take that mandate very seriously and our more than 15,000 commercial customers of all sizes and industries around the world expect nothing less from us.

The guidance that Chris Komisarjevsky provides in this great new book, *The Power of Reputation,* works and works well. I know firsthand.

When I was named chief executive officer of Ryder in 2000, I never considered myself a typical turnaround manager. Yet, what I knew for sure was that future success depended on my reputation—and that of the company—for being straightforward, trustworthy, and doing what I said we would do. Early on, when asked by investors what I planned to do about growing the company, I was direct. I simply said, "We may have to become smaller, and more profitable, in order to grow in the future." That may not have been what they wanted to hear, but it was the truth.

The following years saw us make numerous business model changes and more than a dozen acquisitions while significantly improving earnings. And, in one of the worst economic periods in history, we generated $614 million in free cash flow, the highest one-year total in the company's nearly eighty-year history.

I've known Chris Komisarjevsky for years. In fact, he is the one I call on when seeking advice on reputation. His background in public relations, communications, and as a successful business leader in his own right have given him the expertise to help guide Ryder in many ways, most often working behind the scenes to ensure that, whatever our challenge, a strong reputation is always at the forefront of our decisions.

I am mindful that I have learned a lot since the early days of my career when I believed that if you simply worked hard and also got the right results the right way, everything else would take care of itself. While there's truth to that, Chris and a handful of others have helped me focus on the importance of communicating and sharing more widely the values I hold dear, and the depth of the personal commitment that I feel toward all those who make Ryder successful. The result is that I tell everyone—both inside and outside the company—that reputation is everything: *Ryder is committed to the sound principles that have made us an industry leader and have helped us earn the trust and confidence of our employees, customers, suppliers, and investors.*

The Power of Reputation is a blueprint for success for everyone. Read this book. And follow it. The key principles of character, communication, and trust form the cornerstone of a strong reputation and success in every career. Authenticity, motivation, confidence, transparency, caring, reaching out, sharing leadership, straight talk, strong values, respect, and integrity are just some of the important building blocks. Follow Chris's practical guidance on how to use those building blocks to construct a more successful career. Keep this book handy to refresh your memory. The principles work for me. They will work for you.

Greg Swienton
Chairman and Chief Executive Officer
Ryder System, Inc. (NYSE:R)

acknowledgments

This book is the product of many talented and wonderful people who gave generously of their time and shared their thoughts because they believe in the power of reputation.

To all of them, my deepest thanks.

First to Greg Swienton, who graciously wrote the Foreword.

And to Ted Athanassiades, Joe Becker, Celia Berk, David Bruce, Chet Burchett, Harold Burson, Vicky Casal, Louis Ciolino, Manny and Lily Dominguez, Richard Edelman, Jettie Edwards, Pat Ford, David Fox, Leslie Gaines-Ross, Michele Galen, Kevin Goldman, Per Heggenes, Alberto Ibarguen, Steve Joenk, Bill Kearns, Margery Kraus, Christophe Lamps, John Maltese, Rose Mann, Dan Neuharth, Claude Ritman, Harvey Rosenthal, Gary Schpero, Bill Segal, Marilyn Thalmayr, and Bob Williamson... all of whom allowed me to capture their words or thoughts. To Linda Hersh, who will always be in our memories. And to two of my mentors, Bill McCaffrey and Phil Callanan.

To Ellen Kadin, whose guidance on the book concept was critical.

To Mark Murray, an outstanding editor, who provided me with insights and discipline.

To Jennifer Holder, a terrific editor, whose thinking guided the structure of the final manuscript and its design.

To the many colleagues with whom I've had the chance to work and from whom I have learned so much.

And to my wife, Reina, and all my children for their patience and understanding as I often spent hours from dawn to well into the night at the keyboard.

Thank you.

the power of reputation

introduction

Reality, Perception, and Your Most Powerful Asset

Regard your good name as the richest jewel you can possibly be possessed of. . . . The way to gain a good reputation is to endeavor to be what you desire to appear.

—Socrates

AS THE SUMMER turned to fall I took my car to the dealership for repairs. The weather was just starting to turn cold and I just didn't like the sound when I turned the key and the battery started to crank the engine. "No time like the present," I thought. I wouldn't feel right if my wife, Reina, or one of my kids needed to use the car and it wouldn't start, especially if they were by themselves.

When I spoke with Louis Ciolino, the lead service consultant I always ask for, I tried politely to let him know how important it was that the battery be tested and, if even just starting to go bad, be replaced. To Louis, this could have been an unimportant request that he didn't have to take seriously. But I had hardly started to talk, expressing my concern, when Louis looked up from his computer and said, "I haven't changed my face in 30 years."

Yes, Louis does have an interesting way of phrasing things. But I knew exactly what he meant. Over the years, he's never changed his priorities: to remain customer focused and caring. Needless to say, Louis takes pride in what he does. He is a professional and is one of those remarkable guys who knows his customers by first name. He never needs much more than that in order to recommend the best course of action.

This time was no different.

Louis knows what it takes to build a solid reputation for service. He knows it means working hard, being personally committed, and building relationships. Most of all, he knows that he has to be trusted, not just for one day or one service visit, but for the long run.

This is the reality behind his reputation. He has earned it through offering true service in a friendly way that everyone appreciates. That's why so many of us keep asking for him, why we tell our friends and acquaintances about him, and why his career is successful.

Reputation Is Powerful

I'm no different from any other guy who brings his car in for repairs. But I am assured of quality and can avoid the apprehension that many experience because I simply take my car to Louis.

As a public relations professional, professor, board member, manager, volunteer, combat veteran, and, most of all, a father, I am acutely aware of the importance of reputation. And I'm not alone in doing so—people everywhere keep their ears to the ground and follow up when they get a good recommendation. If their first, second, and third experience with someone demonstrates that there is reality behind a reputation, they will continue doing business there. Moreover, when trust is there and proven over time, they may even ask for new services, expanding the relationship. Everyone, in turn, benefits from the increased business.

Over the years, I've been fortunate to have had the opportunity to speak with people at all professional levels and in different types of organizations about their views on reputation. In those conversations, I've never been able to resist the temptation to ask a very simple question: "Do you believe that reputation is important?"

The answer often comes quickly. While holding back a slight chuckle— or maybe a laugh—they say, "Of course." Some might punctuate their reply by rolling their eyes, while others just look at me quizzically. I sense that more than a few of them seem to think that just asking the question means that I must have been living on the moon.

When I push for an answer, no one minces their words. They come right out and tell me that, if anyone thinks reputation isn't important, they must be crazy.

Perhaps the fact that they are so direct and blunt is because they took the time and effort to build reputations that have withstood the pressures, endured good times and bad, and continued to serve as the foundation for their success. Or perhaps a few have even learned the hard way that a loss of reputation or unwillingness to live up to a commitment and fulfill a promise can prove to be the leading edge of a major problem, if not advance warning of a looming collapse. When I ask them to rate reputation on a scale of importance, from one to five, it always rates high. Some tell me that it is the most important—number five—while others rank it at number four. It seems everyone agrees that reputation is at or near the top when it comes to the ability to be successful.

Clearly, reputation is among our most treasured and powerful assets. At its simplest, it is what others think of us. This simple fact affects everything we do, everything we say, everyone around us, and everything we try to accomplish . . . private and public, personal and professional.

For some, reputation makes the difference between success and failure. For others, it closes the gap between mediocrity and success by creating special opportunities to move beyond the ordinary and accomplish the extraordinary. For still others, it offers a unique advantage to overcome challenges that otherwise might have been considered daunting or even impossible.

In my experience, on the road to success there is nothing more important than reputation when it comes to a strong foundation on which we build our relationships, decisions, achievements, and careers.

Think of the way reputation affects the way you relate to the businesses and organizations in your life. We judge organizations much the same way we judge the people around us. We look them in the eye, listen to what they say, notice what they don't say, watch how they behave, and then we make our judgments. Subconsciously, we ask ourselves: Do we think they can be trusted? Do we think they are reputable? Do we think they will do what they say, and do we think that what they do will be meaningful? We ascribe human values and characteristics to every kind of organization—whether a for-profit or a not-for-profit. We use our answers to decide whether we want to relate to that organization, whether through buying a product or service, investing in them, or taking them on as a vendor or client.

How we perceive, and therefore describe, those organizations can vary dramatically. The words we use to describe them are the ones that most often relate to our own values. When we think well of a company or an organization and have a positive view of the values that underlie its decisions, we use endearing human terms such as "good," "warm," "fair," "ethical," "responsible," "trustworthy," and "personable." Or we describe an organization as one that "we like" and "treats us well."

When it is an organization we don't like, our descriptions turn nasty: "doesn't care," "takes advantage of us," "rips us off," "is dishonest," "misuses our donations," "is unfair," and "chases the almighty buck at our expense."

To look at this from a completely different perspective, I asked some of the people I've interviewed over the years to tell me what kind of animal comes to mind when they think of some of the more widely recognized companies. The answers were pretty graphic and telling. When they said "snake," it spoke volumes of what they thought about a company's integrity and honesty. Companies that were described as a lion or a tiger suggested a reputation for aggressive competition. Sharks conjured up images of financial avarice and ruthless behavior, with no compassion or regard to the success of others. At the same time, puppies and house cats were descriptions of kinder, gentler companies whose business activity was mild, well meaning, pleasant, a Ma-and-Pop shop—and perhaps even easily taken advantage of by ruthless companies.

It doesn't take much thought to realize that these reactions to the reputations of a range of companies tell an important story about our own reputations as individuals. Reputation often has its base in an emotional first reaction. It might be a gut response, based on what action has been taken or what words have been communicated. The truth is that whether or not a reputation has grounding in actions and experience, at the core of reputation is simply *a feeling or a belief.*

This is why reputation can seem to be so hard to control or manage. Its root is in the nebulous realm of emotions, in each person's feeling about you or your organization. The good news is that the seeds of a good reputation are identifiable, and you can plant those seeds so that positive roots will grow and positive experiences will flower. Plant the right seeds and success is yours.

Celia Berk, chief talent officer for Young & Rubicam Group, is often called upon to help people with their professional development. She explains it this way:

> I tell them that they are the ones who must "manage" their own careers. That includes their reputations inside and outside the organization.
>
> Most importantly, as they manage their careers and reputations, they must remember that their actions have consequences. If there are inconsistencies, there is little credibility.

Reputation Is Your Most Important Asset

If there is one message in this book to remember, it is just this: In every facet of our lives, reputation is among our most treasured and powerful assets.

I intentionally choose to describe reputation as an asset, simply because an asset is anything we own that has exchange value. This point is important.

Think of it from two perspectives.

First of all, we own our reputation. Whether or not we feel we deserve it, the responsibility for the views of us that have taken shape in other people's minds falls on us and us alone. When we take responsibility, when we "own" our reputation—that is the moment we can do something about it, when we can begin to consciously shape it.

Second, as an asset, reputation has an exchange value. We engage in active exchanges based on our reputation—either attracting business, attention, or support from those around us, or repelling it. Revenue climbs, we earn a promotion, we land a long-term client, or we negotiate great terms with a vendor we also respect. Or none of those things happen.

Margery Kraus is founder and chief executive of the worldwide consulting firm APCO Worldwide, which developed a Return on Reputation

Indicator and Index in partnership with the Retail Industry Leaders Association. Here's what her research shows on the power of reputation to affect the bottom line.

> Our Return on Reputation research demonstrates that "doing the right thing" is also "the right thing to do for business" . . . just as we know that "doing the right thing" is so important to our success as individuals. One of the interesting aspects of this research is that it directly tracks the linkage from behavior to perception to action. Using the retail industry research as an example, there is a direct correlation between perceptions—those met, not met, or exceeded—and the bottom line.
>
> In any kind of reputation research, the underlying principles are no different than those that determine the success of our own careers. Through all of the work I have done with different organizations—from trade associations to social service organizations, and from governments to corporations—the data consistently show that reputation and meeting expectations are key.

As you delve into this book, consider what your own reputation goals are—what is your personal bottom line? Are you looking to build a business? Do you want to earn a promotion? Lead a team effectively? Widen your network of potential clients? Grow sales? Attract quality vendors and allies?

All these things are possible when you have a positive reputation because it is a major determining factor in the choice that people make when considering their options. More often than not, your good reputation is the reason they choose you.

True to Life

Our words and actions can build or tarnish our own reputations as well as the reputations of those around us. This book shares what I have learned and what I have practiced. The ideas here apply to people across all types and sizes of organizations and in all fields. They include corporate employees, independent business owners, consultants, entrepreneurs, contract workers, and freelancers.

You can build and improve on these concepts as they work to make your own career more successful.

This book is a simple one. It's not theoretical. It's a practical career guide for those who wish to succeed in the workplace, in any role or type of business. The book is straightforward, practical, and concise, written to give you clear instruction on how to create a reality of service based on values, how to communicate those values, and how to build relationships based on trust.

In writing this book, I spoke with friends and colleagues whose reputations I admire and whose careers are successful in good measure because of their character, the decisions they make, the priorities they set, their ability to communicate, and the trust others place in them. I sought out the real-life experiences of people who have demonstrated their success—from profit to nonprofit, from trade associations to foundations, and from charities to healthcare providers.

Having been in public relations, a profession in which reputation is the focus of my work, I have also used my experience as a catalyst for bringing a range of ideas together in the hopes that you can learn from what successful businesspeople have done and how they have behaved.

Three Critical Factors: Character, Communication, and Trust

This book puts forth the idea that reputation is our most powerful asset and is vital to our success. In my experience, reputation is based on three critical factors, as illustrated in Figure I-1.

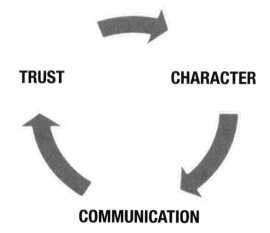

TRUST **CHARACTER**

COMMUNICATION

Figure I–1. The three critical factors of reputation.

Character is who we are and what we value. Communication is how we share our thoughts and values, engage and learn from others, and reach out to help in any way we can. Character, followed by Communication, leads to Trust, which generates the support and allegiance that lead to a positive Reputation. Trust is the direct result of who we actually are and how we actually behave. This connection—from Character, to Communication, to Trust, to Reputation—is the path to follow in developing a positive reputation for yourself.

This is the path you will find in this book. It is one you should follow.

The power to create a strong and positive reputation lies in our own two hands. We control what we do and what we say, how we behave and, as a result, how others see us. Reputation is not something that *just happens*. It is up to us. However, it can be molded by others if we don't take charge or just leave it to chance.

You can build the type of reputation that will serve you well. But it must be genuine and lived each day, or it will not stand the test of time. We can't force other people's perceptions, but we can create a positive reality that earns a positive reputation.

As the saying goes, *perception is reality.*

Thankfully, we can be the master of our success if we choose. We can take steps to shape a successful future for ourselves if we behave in a way that underscores our commitment to lasting values, respects those with whom we work, and demonstrates every day that we do what we say.

Remember—lasting values, respect for others, and doing what you say you will do. These are crucial to a strong reputation and success.

This book will help guide you along those steps.

A truly good book teaches me better than to read it. I must soon lay it down, and commence living on its hint. What I began by reading, I must finish by acting.
—Henry David Thoreau

part one

character

Character is like a tree and reputation like a shadow. The shadow is what we think of it; the tree is the real thing.

—Abraham Lincoln

When we look at our careers, each of us can identify at least one, if not more, instances when we had to make a difficult decision because a situation or opportunity was conflicting with our values. Knowing what our values are, knowing just what we stand for, can make those decisions easier. We know just what to do. And basing these decisions on positive values—which radiate to those in our network of professionals, colleagues, and friends—will earn you a solid reputation.

A firm I was managing was talking with a potential client, a company that *Fortune* consistently ranked within its top 50. This company was on every public relations firm's "to die for" list. We had engaged in discussions with the company for months and had made a number of presentations. The excitement surrounding this client possibility was palpable.

As it became clear that we were one of the top contenders for a long-term relationship, negotiations began in earnest. We talked through how the client relationship team would be staffed, who would lead the work, how the communication between our team and the client would be designed, what services were to be provided, and what offices and regions in the world were to be included in the assignment.

As details were being ironed out, we sensed that there was an underlying issue that had yet to be fully discussed. For many years, we had been retained by another company, also on an extensive, global assignment. That company was a long and cherished client. We had a very strong professional relationship, and those who worked on this assignment loved the work. It was intellectually challenging and very rewarding.

What eventually came to light was that, in order to be retained by the client with whom we were talking, we would need to resign the client that we had served for so many years. The prospective client felt that, if we continued to work for our current client, it would be a conflict since some of its business operations were in competition.

This created a dilemma for some. They were looking at a new client versus a long-term client. They were excited about what they saw as different opportunities and new excitement in the types of assignments. Potential revenue also played a role in their thinking.

In my mind, there was little doubt. I spoke with the founder of our firm to get his view. It confirmed my own. And we politely declined further discussions with our prospective client.

Why was this decision so clear? It came down to a sense of values, one of which was loyalty. We had worked closely with our client for years. We had weathered all sorts of storms together. We were trusted. And, as a consulting firm, we had a long tradition of loyalty to our clients. We wanted them to know they could count on us and we wanted new clients to feel the same way. If we had dropped our long-standing client, what kind of message would that have sent to everyone else we served? Trust would have been broken, doubts would have crept into our dealings, and relationships would have suffered.

Our decision was based on values we held dear. That fact made the decision easy and made our priorities clear to everyone.

chapter 1

This Is the Era of Personal Character

In my lifetime, American business has never been under such scrutiny. To be blunt, much of it is deserved.
—Henry Paulson, Jr., speaking when a senior executive at Goldman Sachs.
He went on to become the U.S. Secretary of the Treasury.

GONE IS THE DAY when the world worked according to one famous advertising slogan of the 1960s: "A title on the door rates a Bigelow on the floor." In fact, these days just having a title on the door doesn't really get you very far. Neither does a huge salary or even your good looks. Attributes that lie on the surface no longer bring respect, warrant allegiance, deliver loyalty at any cost, or ensure a strong reputation. This is the era in which reputation is earned through the demonstration of a positive personal character.

The most powerful way to build a successful career is through the strength of your personal character. This is at the core of all you do and all you say. It determines the decisions you make and the enterprises you pursue.

We are in an era that has witnessed the demise of industry giants who thought they were above the law, lied to customers and investors, used creative accounting to hide misconduct, earned profit at the expense of everyone associated with them, and in the process destroyed all traces of trust. The collapse of these companies and the downfalls of their executives demonstrate that greed, manipulation, and dishonesty have no place in business. Business leaders who build their reputations on fear and loathing go down in history as failures.

A panel of top business school professors associated with Portfolio.com assembled a list of "The Worst American CEOs of All Time." The panel looked at *the records of CEOs who most effectively destroyed value and innovation while displaying the worst management skills throughout their management tenure.*[1]

Enron founder Ken Lay professed the highest values for his company, and even wrote them down in a values statement for all company employees to follow. But he lived none of them himself—neither in the way he managed his business nor in how he treated his people. The resulting collapse of Enron cost 5,600 people their jobs, wiped out more than $2 billion in retirement savings, and turned an estimated $60 billion in market capital into worthless paper. Also tragic was the immediate and long-term impact that the scandal had on many Americans' willingness to place their trust in other business leaders and feel secure about their own jobs. Just before he died of a heart attack, Lay received a decades-long prison sentence.

Other "worst CEOs" include Dick Fuld of the now-collapsed Lehman Brothers, who tops the list. Bernie Ebbers of WorldCom comes in at number five. There are more: Conrad Black of Hollinger International, Dennis Kozlowski of Tyco, Walter A. Forbes of Cendant, and Bernard Madoff, to name only a few of the more widely known. These leaders all built reputations that, when their real actions and motivations became known, were exposed as little more than "illusions of success." Outwardly, they had the position, the money, the power. But inwardly their values were sawdust. They ultimately did themselves in. Such are the fates and fortunes of people whose priorities and actions are rooted in negative and detrimental motives.

There is a powerful lesson behind "The Worst American CEOs of All Time." These people chose to lead in ways that were doomed . . . doomed because very few people are inspired to follow leaders and managers whose motivations will not stand the test of time.

Character That Works

When I think of an example of someone with great character, I think of a very talented executive who worked for me, Pat Ford. He took charge of one of our business units, which was facing some tough times. In a relatively short time after assuming responsibility for recovery, everything began to turn around. I wanted to know how he was accomplishing the turnaround, and why it was working so well. But Pat refused to take the credit—every time I asked, he gave all the credit to his team.

So I asked his staff members. They certainly gave him credit. They all spoke with great admiration about his personal integrity, his professionalism, and his ability to bring everyone together. When I asked them to describe what he was like in the early stages of the turnaround, they said it was almost as if Pat were standing at the bottom of a hill with a runaway train barreling down toward him. There he was standing right on those tracks, they said, but he didn't give ground. He stood there with clenched fists and defiance on his face. At the top of his lungs, he was yelling, "STOP!" And, in their view, the train did just that.

Pat wasn't anywhere near train tracks. And he wasn't Superman, or Batman, or Spiderman. But his courage to meet the situation head-on made him a hero, and his team loved him for it. They knew that he was always there, out in front. They knew that he was working harder than any of them. And they knew if anyone could make the turnaround happen, it was Pat. And he did.

It was the sheer force of Pat's character and the depth of his commitment that made this possible.

Was it that he was genuine? Was it that he was there when the work needed to get done, partnering with each member of his team? Was it that they all respected him? Or was it that he respected them? Was it that they could trust him? Or was it that he trusted them? Was it that he was a man of his word . . . a person of integrity? From my conversations, I knew that the answers to all those questions were a resounding "Yes."

Everything Pat did, he did with emotion, humility, and feeling.

In return, Pat's team members behaved like his partners, took responsibility, and celebrated success as a group. If things happened to go in the wrong direction, they were willing to share those consequences too. As time went by, each person took a strong sense of ownership, and a unique bond formed between members of the team.

This reflects the magic of having personal character at the heart of your reputation. At the moment when the people you work with are ready to stand up and shout from the rooftops that they strongly believe that something you are doing can and should be done, others will pick it up and follow. The enthusiasm and commitment become contagious. If you have the will to get something done, you will have the support from those who work with you and for you. Your reputation means everything.

Hiring for Character

History tells us that people who have positive character traits create positive results. These days when companies interview candidates for a job or consider them for promotion, many of the questions they ask are angled so that they reveal character. When it comes to getting the job you want, allowing your character to shine through is important.

Ask any human resource professional tasked with taking an active role in counseling a workforce on how to improve and strengthen professional development: they know that character drives everything employees accomplish and, in turn, is a key driver of the success of the business. As Celia Berk, chief talent officer for Young & Rubicam Group, puts it,

> When I interview someone, or review their performance, I look for a strong work ethic, intellectual curiosity, and the courage to stand up for what they believe in. I look for ambition, but not carried out at the expense of others. These are some of the key attributes that make our best performers stand out from the rest. And these qualities are visible early on in someone's career, long before they become a manager.
>
> Every one of our team members is an individual and each of them helps shape our company's reputation. The way each of them behaves is a reflection of the entire enterprise and vice versa.

Reputation by Association

As Berk points out, organizations recognize that there is also a fine line between the reputation of an individual and the reputation of the organization where the individual works. It is people who are the public face of every organization in all interactions, making these two reputations closely aligned. In the same way, individuals can take on the reputation of the organization. For this reason, being conscious of your own reputation means being conscious of the reputation of the organization for which you work and the organizations with which you do business.

There have been countless times when, over the years, college students and recent graduates have asked me for guidance on getting that first job, receiving a coveted internship, or exploring the best way to move on to the next level in their careers. Similar to so many other senior executives, I have always felt it important to take the time to provide whatever guidance I could. For me, invariably, that guidance would focus on one factor critical to success: character, including dedication and hard work.

I remember one time when a very talented young woman, Vicky Casal, came to talk to me about her career and how to make the leap she felt she deserved but found so elusive. The economy was also a factor. Jobs were harder to come by. But she knew it was time to move on. Her core problem was that she was a little too eager to make the move and was close to reacting to her feeling of being trapped in her current position in a way that would not serve her well in her career. The fact that her boss— an entrepreneur—was very hard-driving and aggressive didn't help either. Not only did it make Vicky impatient but, as time went on, she became irritated and less effective at work. Those who knew her also were concerned that some of those negative leadership traits she encountered with her boss might be rubbing off on her.

The challenge Vicky faced was twofold: first, how best to pave the way for a move to a better position; and second, how not to take on the characteristics of her boss. If there is one thing I know from running a business, ruthlessness is not a prized characteristic, nor something that is endearing to anyone, employee or business partner.

When I sat down with Vicky, I explained the importance of character and reputation and what it can do for her. Then we came up with concrete steps that she could take to not only make the most of her current job, but also improve the way she comes across in an interview.

Four Steps for You to Use in Your Career

With Vicky, we developed a four-step plan of action to move her career in a new and more satisfying direction. These four steps can work for you too.

The first step is to adopt the perspective that your current work and its environment are part of an important learning experience. Since Vicky knew that the company was successful, even though the internal environment was a tough one, she focused on her job as a good place to train. She recognized that the company's reputation for award-winning work would be an asset and, if positioned properly, a strong part of her resume. Rather than letting herself be distracted, she started to pour all of her energies into her job.

The second step is to develop strength of character. Vicky knew that she had to summon the courage and strength never to overreact, but simply to learn...always looking at the experience in as objective a way as possible. Does this take patience? Absolutely. Does this take self-control? Of course. Does this take focusing on the right values? No doubt. Clearly, it takes a growing maturity and understanding to focus on what is best and recognize that every situation and every work experience is a building block for the future. With this step, important elements of character can emerge within you like never before.

The third step requires pen, paper, honesty, and insight. Vicky wrote down what she was learning—not only the practical work lessons but, more important at this stage, what she was learning about the importance of values and behavior that would better prepare her for the future. As I suggested for Vicky, I encourage you to turn negative experiences into valuable fountains of insight. We can learn a lot from situations that challenge us, and identifying exactly what we want to glean from them is nothing short of alchemy, turning lead into gold.

From then on, Vicky's search for a new job took on a different cast. Her work skills had been honed by perseverance, and elements of her character had been nurtured by determination. In fact, those elements of character she was honing and becoming conscious of became key points whenever she described herself in her resume, in a cover letter, or in an interview.

The fourth step is the simplest. With time, introspection, and the clarity that such introspection brings, your job search can take a new turn. Begin looking for companies whose values go hand-in-hand with yours, and for environments in which you think you can have an impact. When Vicky did this, her interviews became more directed and impressive because she knew more about herself and where she wanted to work.

In the end, it was Vicky's character and track record of hard work that made it possible for her to land that new job. This can be true for you, too.

Whether you become an employee, a contractor, or otherwise provide products and services to a company, the moment you create a working relationship, the circle of that company's reputation expands to include you. At best, having the company on your resume or on your project or client list will speak volumes for all you can do. But the company's reputation can also cause unforeseen challenges that you may have to make up for with the power of your own character. All you can do is hone your character and be prepared to demonstrate it.

What You Gain Through a Good Reputation

No two individuals are alike. You're not like me and I'm not like you. Yet, we each bring our own unique but equally valuable contribution to the table. You are your own person. Your personal character—demonstrated by your energy, determination, and commitment to success—is one of the strongest building blocks for your future. Its strength will see you through all kinds of challenges and make facing them that much easier.

The key goal in shaping your reputation is to have your personal character stand as a driving force for everything you do and say. At the same time your reputation can have a very important effect on others as well. In essence, you also become a role model.

You might ask yourself how strong character can work for you in your career. In short, the answer is that others will:

I *Believe in you.* Whether you are fresh out of school or a seasoned manager, when people believe in you they pay attention to you. This can come in the form of special training or assignments. It can mean that others carry out your decisions and follow the action steps you outline. When people believe in you, they know you have both their own and the project's best interest in mind. They respond by happily managing, collaborating with, or following what you say and do.

Emulate your commitment and passion. People at any level can be role models. I have known many senior executives who are inspired by someone working under them. When you demonstrate your character over and over again, they know that you are putting all of your energies, talents, and skills to the task. They know you will see things through to the end and tackle even the toughest assignments. You can create a positive outcome by simply showing your commitment and your passion for excellence in everything you do.

See you work hard and work hard, too. Doing any job well means that you don't look at the clock and tick off the minutes. Use time to the fullest. If the assignment means early mornings, late nights, or hours of traveling, then that is what you do. Be sure that whatever needs to be done gets done. Approach each assignment with a positive attitude and a determination to do the best you can. This level of dedication is invaluable to everyone involved—it is contagious. Your coworkers know that if you are pulling your weight, they will have to pull their weight too. Your boss watches what you do and looks at the results. And if you are the boss, your staff will work to keep up and even surpass your efforts.

Respect your judgment. Because your reputation precedes you, people will expect similar results in the future. If you have a track record for making solid business decisions, if you have demonstrated that you have an area of expertise or skill that has proved valuable in the past, they will come to you to hear your opinion and feedback. They respect your judgment. Your reputation means that your words carry weight—and having a strong reputation gives you a head start and the benefit of the doubt.

Want to participate in all your activities. In the best of situations, people will want to participate in everything you do because of their positive experience with you. If your character shines through your activities, not only are you a solid team player, but you will be perceived as a great leader. People will clamor to get on board. And that can lead to successes that build and make your career dreams come true.

Strengthening Your Character

Personal character is what defines you as a unique person. It is what others see as the qualities that you possess as an individual. Even though people with whom you work probably won't ask you directly, what they really want to know is: What kind of person are you? What are you made of? Underneath it all, they want to understand your values, especially integrity, fairness, and respect for others. This is especially true for how you deal with those who may hold different views from your own.

People also have questions about how you make decisions. They want to try to gain a better understanding of the motives that underlie your actions. In essence, people want to know some basic things about you. They want to know what defines you as a person. Why do you do what you do? What do you think of others? Do you genuinely care about doing the best job possible? What are your values? And how do those values translate into actions each and every day, whether you are on or off the job?

Being able to answer these questions for yourself is the first step toward consciously acting on them. The chapters that follow focus on giving you the tools you need to strengthen your character so that it underlies all you say and do.

NOTE

1. Portfolio.com, "The Worst American CEOs of All Time," accessed at www.cnbc.com/id/30502091.

chapter 2

Experiences That Shape Character

Reputation and character aren't always the result of a formal process. They are in part instinctive, perhaps the product of our environment, our family, and our upbringing.

—Harvey Rosenthal, retired president
and board member of CVS Corporation

WHEN I GRADUATED from college and enlisted in the Army, I went from basic training in Missouri to Officer Candidate School in Oklahoma, and then on to helicopter flight school in Texas and Alabama. After graduating from flight school, I was flying Hueys in combat in Vietnam.

Throughout my military officer and pilot training, we focused on character and responsibility. Never have I felt the importance of character and the challenge of responsibility as intensely as when the lives of those soldiers sitting in the back of the helicopter were dependent on me.

Throughout my business career, I have never forgotten what that was like.

There are strong lessons to learn about personal character and responsibility from our life experiences. Being in the military is one of them.

Regardless of the branch of service, the military is not built on the idea that leadership means barking orders and telling others what to do. Of course, it is true that rank has command and that sometimes giving orders gets the job done. Yet, officers are trained first by having to "follow" so that, ultimately, they can lead with an appreciation and understanding of what it is like to walk in the shoes of those who would follow them.

Start at the Beginning

No matter how talented we are, no matter how much we learned in school, and no matter how hard we work, each one of us has to start our career at the beginning. Having pumped gas or driven a tractor, we learn about managing a small business—the local gas station or a hometown landscaping company. Having done the menial tasks, we know how important even the smallest details are to the success of the enterprise. Having sorted the mail, we see the mailroom from the inside, and the skills we develop will help us run the mailroom one day . . . and even the much larger company, as did my close friend Bill McCaffrey, whose career took him literally from the mailroom to the executive suite at AXA Equitable. Although he experienced humble beginnings, the drive he showed from the very first day never stopped. He paved the way for himself and helped so many others in later years as they, too, worked their way up the ladder.

You can't start at the top. In fact, most will likely start at the entry level. By doing that, we learn more. We prove ourselves and we come to understand that it is a good thing to learn the ropes from the ground up.

Work hard at the menial tasks and you will earn a great reputation not only for your work, but as you rise, the people working for you will regard you with respect because you have been in their shoes.

The menial work we need to do to earn our stripes can be an important lesson in character. Steve Joenk, now president and CEO of AXA Equitable Funds Management Group, LLC, relates one of those experiences that for him drove home the importance of starting at the beginning. To him, this was a clear lesson in building his reputation.

> I was a newly minted MBA when I got my first real awakening into how important it was that I took charge of my career and made my reputation my first priority. I had landed a job working for a company

in Chicago and I was sent to one of our factories on the South Side. I'd gone through the customary interview process. Everyone had seen my resume so they knew about me, my education, and my career goals. I showed up, as I thought appropriate, in my suit.

The factory manager welcomed me very warmly and asked if I wanted to hang my jacket up. Of course, I said, Yes. I thought he was being very friendly and wanted me to feel comfortable. No sooner had he hung up my jacket behind the door than he handed me a broom. My first job as an MBA was to sweep the warehouse. Was I shocked? You bet. But I learned pretty quickly that, if I was to be respected, there couldn't be any job that I wouldn't do if it needed to get done. And someone had to sweep the warehouse floor. Why shouldn't it be me?

To this day, that Chicago experience and the relationships that developed have been sources of great pride to me.

By demonstrating his work ethic in a task as basic as sweeping the floors, I am sure that Steve's boss in Chicago saw he had a winner on his hands. And when his new coworkers witnessed him earnestly and cheerfully accomplishing the task—despite the MBA and the suit—their regard for him was positive from the start. His reputation was off to a good start, and that pivotal task of readily sweeping the floor on his first day set his career on the fast track.

If It's Worth Doing, It's Worth Doing Well

Most of us remember being told at least once, "If it is worth doing, it is worth doing well." The most vivid time I heard that adage, the time that froze it in my memory forever, was when I was stationed at Fort Leonard Wood, in the Ozark Mountains of Missouri. I had just enlisted in the Army and was assigned KP duty, more formally known in those days as kitchen patrol. I sat on an old steel chair peeling potatoes at four o'clock in the morning on a dark, damp, and cold October day.

The drill sergeant hollered the saying at me with, as you'd expect, a few expletives and verbal exclamation points. Was his admonition critical to achieving better roasted potatoes for the recruits' breakfast? Not quite. But he was driving home a point and it did register: always do your best, regardless the task or how menial.

One of the most challenging lessons for each of us is that managing our career is up to us. No one will build our careers for us. Just like anything else of importance, we have to take charge and commit to the long term.

Think back to your first job. Perhaps you had a part-time job in high school, working during the evenings, the weekends, the holiday seasons, or for the summers. You applied for the job, received the offer, and the first day arrived. When you walked in the door, it was unfamiliar, perhaps even a little frightening. It was a new experience. Whether or not you realized it at the time, it was the start of your employment record and your working career. From that day on, you had to prove yourself. You had to work hard. If you didn't pass muster, you might have lost the job or, just as final, you weren't asked back to work the next season.

But you have gotten where you are because you work hard and do your job well.

What about that next job search? What does your potential boss or the human resources professional see when he or she looks at your resume?

Many of us who worked our way up the ladder started to work at an early age, perhaps with odd jobs or limited hours during the summer because you were still young and were required to have a "work permit" issued by your school. If you are the one interviewing a candidate or looking at a resume, what does that kind of hard work at an early age tell you about work ethic and desire? What does that say about character and the value you want from your employees?

How do you compare the potential of two candidates, one of whom has worked every summer since the age of 14 and another who has spent summers traveling? Is that really a fair question? Perhaps not in each case, but the work experience certainly does say something about willingness, focus, and disciplined hard work.

That willingness to work hard—shaped at an early age—is a prime indicator of your potential. Not only have you experienced what it is like to get up and go to work on time each day, but you have built a track record showing that you can work and stick to it.

Whether we want to admit it or not, there is an immediate recognition of hard work and trustworthiness for those who start at the bottom and work their way up and those who take on menial tasks with energy and eagerness. That kind of experience is immediately recognized and proves to be a crucial building block for your reputation. On the other hand, complainers and those who arrive late to work on a regular basis don't get too far.

Both reputations have an impact on careers.

As you move along in your career, if you work hard, perform well, and look for increasingly demanding work experiences, the resume you build will be strong and anyone reading it will clearly see the momentum you have brought to your career. Your success will be reflected in a pattern of more and more responsibility.

The Value of Early Experiences

Many successful professionals draw on their early experiences and, if they've risen to an executive level, on their experiences in the field to shape their values. Harvey Rosenthal worked for CVS Corporation for almost his entire career, rising to president, chief executive, and board member. When he started at CVS, the company had forty-five stores. When he retired, the number of stores had reached 1,400. Rosenthal describes the experience that shaped his character and determined the values he instilled in the way CVS does business:

> I spent my first week at CVS as a clerk in the Swampscott, Massachusetts, store. I rang the cash register, unloaded the trucks, and stocked shelves. And on my very first day, my mother and my grandmother happened to walk in that store. Here I was a brand-new Harvard MBA working as a clerk. It gave me a chuckle, but my mom had a proud smile.

> Honestly, I learned a lot in that store that you don't learn in business school.

> So much so that, for years, I made it a point to go back to that Swampscott store to spend the day before Christmas. Especially at that time of the year, you could see, hear, and better understand all the work that store associates, warehouse teams, buyers, and others had to do in order to make for a successful holiday season. It also let me "think like a customer."

Beyond keeping me grounded, my time in the stores set an example and gave me credibility.

My management style was not to tell others what to do but to show them and encourage them to look around to uncover the things they should do to be even more successful. I had been in retail all my life. I started working in my father's shoe store at the age of 10. Quite frankly, a lot of people didn't see what I saw. My challenge was to make it so they could see that same way too. I saw everything through the eyes of the customer . . . ever since I was very young.

Perhaps because of my values, I created the slogan for all of us at CVS: "Think like a customer. Act like an owner." It was simple. The concept was twofold. First, you strive for the same thing that a customer wants . . . products in stock and easy to find, fair prices, pleasant staff, and quick checkout. Second, you always ask yourself, "What if I owned the business? What would I do?" The answer would be . . . satisfy the customer—he or she could get the same products somewhere else—honor the coupon, give the refund, and smile.

A First Exercise in Character

Take a moment to look back at your life. What experiences have made you who you are? What experiences have shaped the way you act and the decisions you make? They can be from your business experience or your life experience. Maybe you were volunteering for a worthy cause. Perhaps it was a major life event, like the birth of your children. It could even go back to childhood and a playground experience.

Take out a pen and paper and list them. Then, for each of these experiences, write down your responses to the following questions:

I *What was the situation?* Begin by describing the situation you were in. Describe the company, the environment, why you were participating, why the situation was important. Basically, write down all the relevant background information. This could be important now, as you find similar situations in which you can apply the lesson to character.

❙ *What happened?* Write down what happened during that experience with as much detail as you can. Walking through the events might even trigger further insight than you originally thought. Include what you said, what others said, how you dealt with the situation, and even how someone else reacted.

❙ *What did you feel?* The strongest motivational experiences are rooted in powerful emotions. Include the feelings you experienced then, in the moment. Also be sure to include what you feel now, in hindsight. Something that may have felt embarrassing or humbling then may inspire you to feel appreciation now.

❙ *What lessons did you learn?* Write down the character lessons that immediately come to mind. Then, look even deeper at your description of what happened. Was there something happening that you weren't previously aware of? Is there some lesson you learned and recognize now, even if you weren't totally conscious of it at the time?

❙ *Have you applied these lessons at other times?* If you have applied what you learned through this experience before, write those instances down. Did the character trait help or hinder the situation? If it helped, describe the situation and tell the story of what happened. Not only does this give you evidence of a strong and positive character trait, it also helps you make the case for why you do the things you do, which can be shared with others. If it hindered, ask yourself: Why? Was the time or place wrong? Is there a way for you to demonstrate your character more effectively?

❙ *How are these lessons applicable to your life now?* Look at your life now, personal and professional, and see if you can apply one of the character traits you learned.

Through this process, we come to value our own character. We can see the positive qualities we express, and by becoming aware of who we already are, we can build on them and make use of them. We can even use our personal story to make the case for a values-based activity or decision. If you do, people will better know where you are coming from, they will respect the story as the foundations for your personal judgment, and most of all, they will understand both you and the situation better. As we will explore in Part Two, which deals with communication, people are more likely to form a good perception of something they understand. By understanding yourself, you can help others understand you in turn. This all builds a terrific reputation as an authentic person with character and values rooted in real-life experience.

Here is an example of an experience that shaped how a leading businessman came to understand the importance of reputation. Alberto Ibarguen is president and chief executive of the John S. and James L. Knight Foundation, whose assets exceed $2.5 billion, making it one of the larger private foundations in the United States.

> In my career, the importance of trust was clear from my first days as a Peace Corps volunteer. After college and before law school, I joined the Peace Corps and my first assignment was in Venezuela. I realized quickly that, when people looked and listened to me, I was, in effect, also the United States. From the start, what I did, what I said, and how I behaved was a reflection of both me and the U.S. If those in Venezuela didn't trust the U.S., they didn't trust me. And, if they didn't trust me, they didn't trust the U.S. It was almost scary . . . how intertwined my personal behavior and my professional life was from that point on.
>
> It didn't stop there. It's been that way ever since. When I walk into a room, the lines are blurred. I am not just a publisher. I am not just a lawyer by training. Nor am I simply manager of the Knight Foundation. I am all of the above—and I am an individual. Each stage of my life has created a certain perception of who I am, what I stand for, and whether I can be trusted. Those perceptions carry forward to each new stage of my career.

Role Models Who Have Helped Shape Who You Are

Another way of shaping our character is to learn from others. Who has been a role model to you? Most of us have had a number of role models in our lives. Some are within our family—especially relating to values and work ethic—and others are in the work environment.

Parents often head the list. My parents filled that role. Out of necessity when my father died, my mother, one of the early pioneers in modern dance, relied on her reputation to support the family by building her dance studio business, at which she taught others the techniques of Martha Graham and Doris Humphrey. Day after day, in spite of the fact that my brother and sister were still young, she conducted classes, sharing her love of dance and encouraging her students to put their hearts, souls, and muscles into something important to them. Watching some classes after school, I saw early on the passion and caring that she put into her work and the impact that it had on her students. My own father's relentless push to bring new ideas to theaters and on-stage through dramatic sets, architecture, costume design, and acting demonstrated a drive that gave his life a special meaning. Following my father's death, my mother remarried and I watched with awe how my stepfather, a newspaper columnist and writer, had the patience and determination to sit at his Smith Corona typewriter and write 700 words per day, six days every week. Published in hundreds of papers around the country, his column was adored by readers and never did he miss filing his column by 3:30 each afternoon.

That mixture of love, passion, and determination shone through. They were character building-blocks that live with me every day.

On the work front, when I started as a junior account executive in the public relations agency business, I worked for a wonderful man, Phil Callanan, who was in charge of our editorial services department. One evening, late at night, when you could look out the window to the north and see the red dots of the taillights on the cars moving up 3rd Avenue in New York City, I remember giving Phil the copy for a brochure I was writing for a client. I sat in front of his desk while he paced around the room after reading my draft. It seemed like an eternity. Finally, he returned to the desk and pointed to one single word in the middle of page four. He simply said to me: "Chris, this is not the right word." I didn't know what to think. Out of pages of copy, he only picked out one word to comment on. I just didn't understand. So, I asked him; "Why?" It took him another long time to answer. He finally said: "I don't know, Chris. All I know is that it isn't the correct word." What Phil was teaching was that there are times when you sense something isn't right but you may not really know why. In your stomach, you just know it isn't right. And, even though you may not be able to explain it, you need to trust your gut. Yes, in this case, the English language is full of connotations and denotations and the word was undoubtedly one of those, but Phil was telling me much more. This was a lesson for life and careers.

These lessons are the foundation of values, of character, and of reputation.

Have you witnessed a situation in which someone you admire responded in a way that has had a meaningful and profound impact on your career? We are fortunate if we have both mentors and champions who play key roles in helping us build our careers and guide our reputation.

Role Models You Can Seek Out

In my experience, there is a distinction between mentors and champions. Both are key to success, but they play different roles in our professional growth and learning. Mentors are those who help us learn the skills we need to do the job well and whose career guidance can often span our entire career. They are a vital resource and oftentimes a role model, someone with whom we can speak freely and who can show us how to work more efficiently, more productively, and with better tangible results.

Champions are those where we work who take us under their wing and help create new career opportunities, different assignments, and even promotions. They are strong internal advocates for us. They most often push us forward based on what they see as our capabilities and potential. Often, they are in more senior leadership and managerial roles so they can anticipate how we can best prosper and grow in the organization. Or they are entrepreneurs like us, but have established their business at a level to which we aspire.

The challenge we all face is identifying those who could be the mentors and champions who will provide us with the kind of guidance in our careers that will make a profound difference.

When you think about mentors, think about those who will take the time to share with you what you are doing well and where you need to improve. They need to be candid and genuine. And in a way they need to be teachers who care enough to go out of their way so that you learn. You need to see them as experts who, even when their advice is blunt and bold, have much to offer if we care to listen. Sometimes, we learn the most from tough encounters and we must never shy away from them.

When you think about champions, think about those who can be your advocate for either of two reasons: one, they are in a position to know what is going on in the organization and can identify opportunities for you; or two, they are sophisticated and experienced at navigating through an organization's internal management and politics. Like mentors, champions, too, need to care.

How do you reach out to them? Whether you are in a large organization or a small one, the answer is the same: Ask for a time to talk, ask for guidance, be humble, and ask if he or she is willing to take the time to help you learn and grow. Don't be shy. Reach out. Those who would be strong mentors and champions will be more than ready to respond.

A Second Exercise in Character

I strongly encourage you to think about the people whom you admire, whether they are a part of your past or your present. What are the character traits that inspire you? Have you seen them act in ways that motivate you to act in the same way? If so, write down the situation and probe both why they acted as they did and the resulting impact. Doing so will provide insight that will help you with your own actions and motivations, ensuring that your behavior communicates to others in ways that build a solid reputation.

As you think about something they did, hold your own "post-mortem." Do for yourself what many senior managers do when they hold post-mortem discussions in which a team critiques its own performance and team members ask themselves some tough, probing questions about teamwork, preparation, and implementation of programs. Some organizations even conduct follow-up research to learn if a particular initiative actually attained its goals.

You can engage in a post-mortem process with any experience you have. It can be business, it can be personal, but it is guaranteed to be powerful. Gear your post-mortem toward character by probing into how values came into play, and the role that character played in your actions.

Start by writing things down. What do you think you did well? What not so well? When you are candid with yourself, your answers will surprise you . . . and they will be the building blocks for change.

Follow these three steps and answer the questions honestly:

1. Ask "Why?"—Why did you do what you did? What was your motivation?

2. Ask for the "What?"—What were you trying to accomplish? Was your approach the correct one? What did actually happen? What was the outcome? What did it say about you and your values?

3. Ask "How?"—How would you do it if you could do it over again? How would you change things? How can you make that kind of change? How can you ensure that the right values are part of making this change?

After you have asked yourself these questions, think about what the answers tell you about your values and your behavior. And, just as important, think about what guidance your answers provide for the way you will behave in the future.

Feedback on How Your Character Is Perceived

Most organizations require formal performance reviews on a regular basis, at least annually and sometimes more often, perhaps every six months. Too often, though, people see the review as an irritant, rather than a constructive opportunity to learn how you are seen by others.

Use the review in a constructive way and make the most of the opportunity to both demonstrate, and gather feedback on, your character. Here are some ways to do this:

❙ *Plan ahead for the review.* Write down your strengths and weaknesses. Identify what you think you do well and not so well. Be candid. Your candor will be seen by your boss as constructive and will position you as someone who wants to learn, not someone who is defensive.

❙ *Ask for the review.* Don't wait for your boss or the human resources department to talk to you. Be there first. Let them know you want the review and the feedback so that you can improve. Every opportunity like this is a learning experience and a chance to demonstrate your loyalty and willingness to grow.

❙ *Participate actively in the review.* Don't just sit there and let your boss do the talking. Ask questions. Be specific. Ask for guidance. Be eager and open to ideas. Directly ask about values and character. A good question would be, "What are the five words that you would use to describe how you see the values and character I bring to my job?"

I *Ask for additional training.* Look for opportunities to be part of additional training from either inside the organization or by taking courses elsewhere. New ideas and new training will open new doors.

I *Look to next steps.* Let your boss know the value of feedback and that you appreciate the time. Most of all, set a follow-up meeting to gauge progress against new milestones.

On an informal basis, there are other opportunities for you to get feedback on your character. You might have some private time with a boss and mentor—or even a peer—to ask about how you are perceived within the group, department, or company you work with. Travel time, conversation over a meal, and while walking together after a meeting are all prime opportunities for an informal evaluation that can lead to further learning and self-improvement.

Don't Shy Away from 360-Degree Feedback

Beyond a supervisor's informal efforts and individual counseling, one of the most widely used evaluation and review processes is the 360-Degree Feedback Review. With participation from both subordinates and supervisors, the process gives a range of people with whom you work the chance to comment on, and provide their insights into, your skills, teamwork, values, and performance. The review is also seen as an effective tool for self-improvement and as a guide for areas in which additional training and experience could be valuable.

From my perspective, the most interesting aspect of the 360-Degree process is that it can give you a very real sense of how you are perceived by others. In effect, they are commenting not only on your job performance but also on something far broader and equally important to your career development—your reputation. Having personally been part of numerous 360-Degree Feedback Reviews, I think they should be renamed: 360-Degree Reputation Reviews.

The composite picture produced by the review reveals more about trust, follow-through, reliability, compassion, sharing, and team-building than does a standard performance review. It also says how well you give credit to others and how well you communicate throughout the organization.

Just as important—yet too often overlooked—is the opportunity for the 360-Degree Review to help you shape your own professional reputation and the way others view you. The 360-Degree Review process may not be the same as putting together strategic, operating, and financial plans for the success of your company, but it is just as vital for your success. It takes a tremendous amount of objectivity and discipline. It also requires an introspective view into the values and priorities that are most important to you, a frank comparison between the values you talk about and your own actions, the ability to understand and respond to any discrepancy between the two, and a candid recognition of your personal and professional strengths and weaknesses. Without a doubt, it can be a tough but revealing process. It might even be frightening at times. Yet, it might encourage you to make some career-boosting changes.

After identifying the experiences that have shaped your character and after considering feedback you received about how you are perceived by others, you may begin to notice some major themes emerge. Most likely, those themes are the values that underlie what you have learned.

In the next chapter, you will identify what those values are so that you can be clear about who you are and what you stand for. Once you become aware of that, you will have the foundation in place for the reputation you want to build.

chapter 3

Define Your Values

Competition is tough today. Your values must be clear and front and center in your business. Mark my words, if you run a small business and you don't know your customers well, you will not survive. If they don't respect you and what you stand for, they won't come back. If you don't go out of your way for them, they won't walk through your door again. And the reality is that they will just go elsewhere. They might never tell you why but, if you think back, the answer probably will be pretty clear.

—Manny and Lily Dominguez, husband and wife,
owners of a neighborhood pharmacy in New Jersey

PORTRAITURE WAS the form of painting Vincent van Gogh loved but he had no money to pay the models whom he would have hired to sit for him while he painted. So, he invested in a mirror. He went on to paint at least twenty self-portraits in Paris, moving through colors from somber browns and grays to light yellow, reds, greens, and blues . . . with an Impressionist style that, for him, was as much about a state of mind as it was about technique. This period of his life culminated in one of his most famous paintings, *Self-Portrait as an Artist.* It is a dramatic illustration of how he saw his own reflection.

For me, there are two lessons to be learned from van Gogh, neither of which is the tragedy of his fall into insanity or the taking of a razor to his own ear.

First, even without the money he needed, he found a way to pursue what he loved. A mirror sufficed when models were too expensive. He believed in his talent and wouldn't let anything stand in his way. He pursued what he thought he would do best. He had determination and drive.

Second, he had the insight to keep looking at himself, changing paints and colors until he was able to capture and illustrate what he really saw. The mirror was the device he used to look at himself and paint portraits. Each self-portrait moved along a path of self-awareness. The colors and paints followed with time.

In our career, we too face something of the same challenges as van Gogh. There are times when our career ambitions are hampered by obstacles; perhaps we aren't granted the budget we feel we need to accomplish our task, or the industry we love, trained in, and built our experience around is not doing well. When we are at a crossroads and need to make a career decision, such as whether to move across the country for a promotion, it is time to look within at who we are. For many of us, this has become a regular part of navigating our business lives as we move along our career trajectory.

What is not so obvious is that it is only after we look in the mirror and truly see ourselves that we can begin to shape others' perceptions of us. What we see in the mirror is what others can see too. If we want to change how we are perceived, we need to go to the source: we need to look at ourselves. Then we can paint an authentic portrait for others to witness, and that portrait becomes our reputation.

We all need to look at the portrait we paint and ask ourselves if it represents who we are, who we want to be. As you will read later, authenticity is a sure way to build a reputation that stands the test of time. If we want to be successful, that picture must be an accurate portrayal of our character. If it isn't, we need to do something to change that, or success will be either fleeting or nothing more than a dream.

The only way we will be able to be authentic is if we like what we see.

So, what does it take to ensure that you're satisfied with your "reputation portrait"?

In this chapter, I'm going to walk you through a process that will help you get to the core of who you are by helping you define your values. We're going to explore how values affect everything you say and do—especially the decisions you make. And at the end of the chapter, I'm going to ask you to write a personal values statement. Then, in the rest of the book I can help you build on your values to project an authentic image of yourself, which in turn will help people perceive you as you are.

The Magic List

Alberto Ibarguen, president and chief exectuive of the Knight Foundation, is crystal clear about the values that underlie his reputation.

> I always try to think about the kind of values I am projecting. Keeping my word is key to being trusted. Behaving with integrity is vital. Never cutting corners on honesty is at the top of the list. And being humble. There is so much we don't know.

Steve Joenk, president and CEO of AXA Equitable Funds Management Group, LLC, has a very similar perspective on the importance of values:

> Reputation is about knowing ourselves and showing our values to those with whom we work. There will undoubtedly be those who don't agree with you but if you are true to your core values—coupled with a sense of humor—you will prevail.

What values do you hold dearest? We start our investigation with a list that comes from The Foundation for a Better Life website, www.values.com. If you go to the website you can click on each value and read a short description, which can help you decide which are most important to you.

Circle or copy down all the values from the following list that you feel are of particular importance to you. You may even want to rank them. If you are tempted to select so many words that you feel overwhelmed, try this: Ask yourself, "If I were in danger of losing my job, what values would I not sacrifice even if it meant I were to be let go?"

Achievement	Good Manners	Patience
Ambition	Gratitude	Peace
Appreciation	Hard Work	Perseverance
Believe	Helping Others	Persistence
Believe in Yourself	Honesty	Practice
Caring	Hope	Preparation
Character	Humility	Purpose
Charity	Including Others	Reaching Out
Class and Grace	Ingenuity	Respect
Commitment	Innovation	Responsibility
Common Ground	Inspiration	Right Choices
Compassion	Integrity	Rising Above
Compliments	Kindness	Sacrifice
Confidence	Laughter	Sharing
Courage	Leadership	Smile
Courtesy	Learning	Soul
Dedication	Listening	Sportsmanship
Determination	Live Life	Spread Your Wings
Devotion	Live Your Dreams	Stewardship
Do Your Part	Love	Strength
Drive	Loyalty	Teaching by Example
Encouragement	Making a Difference	Team Work
Excellence	Mentoring	True Beauty
Foresight	Motivation	Trust
Forgiveness	Opportunity	Unity
Friendship	Optimism	Vision
Generosity	Overcoming	Volunteering
Giving Back	Passion	

So what are the principles that underlie your behavior? Are you surprised? Or does consciously doing the exercise feel aligned with what you knew deep down? Take the time to reread your character exercises from Chapter 2. How do the experiences that shaped your character relate to your core values?

Stories Behind the Values

It is important to recognize that our values can determine or radically change our career trajectory.

Ask yourself: How have the values you circled come into play in your career?

In this chapter, I offer examples of people I have known well who demonstrated strong values and whose careers were stronger because of them. After you read them, ask yourself: *What is my personal story?*

WORK-LIFE BALANCE

Michele Galen was one of my first hires after I was named chief executive. She had been editing and writing for one of the nation's leading business publications and, when I first interviewed her, it was clear from the outset that her experience gave her the kind of insights that would be very valuable to clients. Moreover, she had earned her law degree and, with that training, came a very disciplined and strategic thought process. Within the first year, she had proved herself to be a star. Clients looked for her guidance. She developed background papers on social and legal issues, presented her findings, and assisted clients dealing with issues related to employees, the workforce, and organizational change. She hired a team, was promoted to managing director, and launched a specialty practice in change communications as more and more clients sought her advice.

The practice grew and demands on her time climbed. At the same time, she wanted to spend more time with her family. Michele wanted to strike a balance between time at home to be with her children and time at work to be with her team and her clients.

Her priorities and values were clear. Family was at least as important as work, if not more so, and now, as her children were growing, they needed more of her time.

She came to me with a request: Can the firm make it possible for her to work from home one or two days a week? Can we link her computer so that she could be as productive from home as from the office?

This was a first for us; after all this was still in the middle 1990s and the technology for any sort of remote sharing of documents and electronic commuting was still just gaining a foothold.

But we said yes and found a way.

That simple request paved the way for Michele's next career move. She had been courageous enough to voice the importance of family values and it was that commitment that others saw in her. As her practice grew, her reputation climbed and she was seen as an individual who, from a very personal perspective, understood firsthand the challenges of striking a successful work-life balance. Others wanted to know how she did it. Human resource specialists, in particular, wanted to know how best to implement similar policies in the companies where they worked.

She was sought after by clients, some trying to hire her. Eventually she did leave the firm, joining a global pharmaceutical company where she was named vice president and would cofound and build what would become a 1,500-member women's leadership group that was focused on empowering women employees to have an even deeper impact on the company. A few years later, she was asked to transfer to Europe and take on a global role in communications, often partnering with Human Resources.

Some may have thought that Michele's values and strong commitment to a balance between family and work put her career in jeopardy. But that couldn't be farther from the truth. The fact is that her values became the cornerstone of her career and her advancement.

LEARNING FROM OTHERS

Christophe Lamps worked in our Geneva office. He spoke four languages and quickly became recognized as the "go to" account executive for tough clients. Always gracious, he was impressive when you met him, and that impression lasted forever.

When he walked in the room, it was his height that struck you at first. He was tall and strong . . . you immediately knew he was an athlete. You could picture him skiing the Alps in deep powder snow. And it was his smile and a firm handshake that solidified the relationship.

But it was the time with him in the conference room that really impressed you. He listened intently, waiting patiently for the client to explain the situation. He never interrupted. He took detailed notes and watched the body language. In due time, of course, he would ask his questions and share his thoughts.

His interpersonal skills were very good. He could judge when the client was ready to listen. And he lived the old client-service story about the consultant who was considered the wisest on earth, simply because he listened first and only spoke with careful words long after.

And, when he spoke, he offered thoughts that built on what he had heard. He had listened carefully. The client—the customer—was impressed.

For some this kind of skill is natural. For most of us, it is learned, sometimes by watching others more senior and other times from a harsh experience or two. Christophe had learned from mentors who had been in the office in the early years of his career. He had taken the time to talk to them, ask them how to improve, and then put the advice into action. When you asked him how he did it, he often said that it was tough at first because asking for advice can be a humbling moment. And, he said, it could be embarrassing because you are opening yourself up to criticism. Regardless if the criticism is well-meant or not, it can be hard to hear, even when you know you asked for it.

But Christophe believed that you can't stay the same and expect to grow professionally. So he kept asking others for advice.

And in that advice, he found a way to stand out from the crowd. Success followed.

Values in Action

If you are serious about making your values the basis for a good reputation, once again turn to pen and paper or go to your laptop or touchpad. Write about the results of your self-analysis in order to become clear on where you excel and where you need to improve. How are you living out your values? How are they being challenged? And in what ways are you neglecting what's important to you? Lay out a plan for reinforcing your strengths and moving beyond your shortcomings. Learn from what you do well and the mistakes you have made.

Be sure to keep your notes. If we don't write things down, they don't seem to have the same weight and importance. Plus, these exercises might be forgotten or tossed out of mind, with no opportunity to go back and look at what you said, what you believed, and what commitments you made. I want you to return to these pieces of paper or those computer documents again and again.

Personal Failings

We've all heard stories or read about managers who lose their jobs for reasons that appear to have nothing to do with work performance. Those situations often surround something financial—perhaps a gift accepted when personal values and a strong sense of integrity should have dictated otherwise.

There are many cases of people who made the wrong decision. In a split second, they damaged their reputations, sometimes irreparably.

And it can come about in surprising and sudden ways. I remember once when I was a young reporter for a small-town newspaper. I was sent on an assignment to write about the next day's grand opening and sale on new products being offered at the local hardware store. The owner very proudly showed me a remodeled section of his store, specifically set up to showcase new items for the summer. New BBQ grills, accessories, swimming pool supplies, and outdoor furniture were all shiny and on display. While answering my reporter's questions, he picked up a newly introduced electrical BBQ grill lighter and handed it to me. He asked me if I wanted it. At first, I didn't know why he would want to just give it to me. And then, I figured it out: perhaps it might have something to do with the story I was writing and whether that story might find its way to the front page of tomorrow's paper. Needless to say, that BBQ grill lighter never left the store that day and the story never made the front page.

But these things do happen. The challenge we face is to be careful and always ask ourselves if something we are about to do would violate our sense of values and put our futures in jeopardy.

The Values Test

Now, let's put your values to the test to ensure that the reputation you build for yourself is real and enduring. Like any other task that requires us to look closely and objectively at our own actions and motives, the tougher it is, the better off you will be in the end. The questions that follow reflect true-to-life situations you could find yourself facing. They cut to the core of values and our character. Answer them as honestly and as thoroughly as you can.

QUESTION 1
Would I be tempted, even to a minor degree, to shade the facts?

Why ask yourself this question?
This question looks for and measures your strength of conviction. Are your values just words or are they principles you live by without compromise? Too often, people espouse the kinds of values that they think others want them to have or others want to hear. But, if those values are not genuine, they won't withstand the onslaught of tough challenges. What happens if your boss behaves in a way that is not in keeping with your values? Do you stand your ground or do you conform and change? The fact is that people are smarter and more perceptive than others sometimes give them credit for. They can see through any values that are not genuine or that are merely opportunistic. With time, they can tell if your values are real or just contrived.

QUESTION 2
What are my relationships like with my coworkers, team members, bosses, and clients? Do I respect them and what they do? Do I think I am better, more talented, or more important than the others? Have I ever wielded authority—at any level—in an inappropriate manner to make things easier or better for myself?

Why ask yourself this question?
This question probes your respect for and willingness to listen to others. It forces you to think about whether you want the best from the people you work with, including their ideas and their growth as individual professionals, or you simply want others to do your bidding. The fact is that teamwork and shared goals are keys to successful business operations. As the saying goes, *there is no "I" in team.*

QUESTION 3

When the project is completed and successful, who gets the credit? Am I comfortable sharing the credit?

Why ask yourself this question?

The people who work with and for you will work harder and more effectively if they know you share praise, give them credit for their work when it is well done, and are in their corner when results are less than successful. Equally important, it is the right thing to do. This question looks to see if you operate with a large ego that takes credit at the expense of others or if you can step to the side and share the praise.

QUESTION 4

What happens if the job doesn't go well? Am I looking for someone to blame? Or do I look at myself first? What responsibility do I consider mine when it comes to working with others?

Why ask yourself this question?

This question probes whether you can handle the pressure and consequences of a project or initiative not working out quite the way you planned. Do you stand up and shoulder the responsibility? Or do you pass the blame along to someone else? Do you take the time to closely scrutinize your performance under pressure? Do you demonstrate caring for others by looking at the skills of the individual team members and putting into place a plan to improve and develop those skills? Everyone makes mistakes, including you and me. But how we respond to those mistakes is a key measure of our reputation and long-term career success.

QUESTION 5

Am I comfortable engaging in a dialog with those who work with me? Am I able to work in a culture where differing views stimulate idea exploration and new approaches? Am I genuinely interested in hearing opinions and ideas that are different from mine? Can I take criticism from those who work with me?

Why ask yourself this question?

This question helps you think through and determine your degree of openness to hearing ideas about how you and your coworkers can work better together. Many people are not comfortable with productive conflict or differing ideas. In the process of avoiding them or even shutting them down, they let invaluable opportunities for brainstorming and creativity pass them by. The fact is that one-way discourse is hardly a conversation, let alone a productive dialog on making continual improvements. New ideas—from all sources—are the key to progress, growth, and success, and the hallmark of someone who earns a positive reputation.

QUESTION 6

Am I comfortable sharing power and authority or do I want it all for myself? Will I also pick up the shovel and dig ditches, especially if that is what I ask others to do?

Why ask yourself this question?
A challenge for many, especially in positions of power, is to share that power and authority. Those who are unable to do so want to be the boss and only the boss. They distance themselves from those they work with and, in the process, lose the allegiance of the very people they need in order to be successful. In any enterprise, follow the example of the best military officers, who lead from the front in battle but wait at the back of the chow line until the entire platoon is served. This question forces you to think whether you are that kind of team member or leader. The best way to earn respect and reputation is to be willing to participate in a group's common goal, in whatever way you can.

QUESTION 7

Am I personally vested in my organization's success or am I just putting in the time? Am I consistently positive in my emotions and my dedication to the organization and the quality of its products or services?

Why ask yourself this question?
At various stages of our careers, we must be reflective and decide if we still have our hearts in the game. This question drives to the core of that issue. Can you look at the job with a fresh perspective? Does it still hold learning opportunities or other new experiences for you? If not, it might

be time to consider other organizations and new challenges. Staying will do little to improve the organization and certainly nothing to bolster your reputation. The fact is that others notice and take their cues from you. As the saying goes, If you are no good for yourself, you are no good for anyone else.

QUESTION 8

Do I probe to understand "why" and "how" things need to get done or am I simply pushing for immediate results?

Why ask yourself this question?
It might be much simpler only to focus on "what needs to get done." However, it is much more challenging to try to understand "why" and "how" those things need to get done and even more challenging to try to understand how to get them done well consistently and over time. This question helps you explore whether you are inquisitive enough and have the intellectual curiosity that will enable you to identify new ideas or strategies that make it possible for you to stand out from the crowd and move up the ladder more surely than some of your contemporaries. It is also the question that forewarns your doom if you focus on short-term gain over long-term and repeatable success.

QUESTION 9

Do I listen carefully to my coworkers, bosses, and clients, or just nod when others are talking? When I work with staff in my department, do I simply tell them what to do or do I prompt strategic thinking by asking questions so they can discover the solutions for themselves?

Why ask yourself this question?
The best leaders are also teachers and role models. And the best of teachers and role models are also the best of listeners and drivers of self-motivation. This question looks to see if you have some of those "teaching" qualities so that those who work with you can, themselves, become managers and leaders by thinking and acting more proactively, gaining more and more responsibility. The Socratic method helps individuals learn far more and far better for the long run.

QUESTION 10

Do my actions mirror my words and is my behavior consistent? Do I behave differently at the workplace, at home, or on the golf course or tennis court?

Why ask yourself this question?

This question challenges whether you really are credible in what you say and what you do. Are you consistent in your core values? Do you do what you say, or does your behavior lag far behind your words? There can be no credibility and therefore no worthy reputation if the two don't follow each other closely, whether you are at work, at home, or at play.

QUESTION 11

Am I ready and eager to start from scratch by meeting the challenges that come from each new assignment? Am I prepared to prove myself at each stage of my career by learning new skills and approaches?

Why ask yourself this question?

Here, the question probes your ability to move successfully through assignments and ultimately through your career. Senior managers will tell you that moving up the ladder and gaining more success means constantly mastering new horizons of learning: new skills, greater maturity, deeper understanding, and a new level of sophistication. It is like starting from scratch with each new assignment or job, each one more challenging than the last.

QUESTION 12

Can people trust me to support them? Do I empower them? Do they know and believe that I am there for them?

Why ask yourself this question?

Above all, are you trustworthy? There are very few qualities more important than trust. Can you meet that standard? If not, there can be no success.

Building and shaping your reputation with trust and character is your most important task. No one can build my reputation for me, and no one can build your reputation for you. Simply put, your reputation is your job.

It cannot be delegated or left to chance. You alone are accountable for what you say, how you say it, what you do, how you do it, and why you do it. You are responsible for your actions, and you are responsible for the consequences. As my wife's mom often told her, and she in turn reminds our children, "The decisions you make dictate the life you lead." Now that you have answered the tough questions and put yourself to the test on paper, you will be better prepared to face the challenges that life throws at you.

Writing a Declaration of Your Values

When I was worldwide chief executive of Burson-Marsteller, decisions about clients often found their way to my desk—which to work with, which to decline politely, and which relationships should come to an end. As the senior manager of the firm, a critical component of my role was clearly to focus on reputation and how our actions would be seen by others.

After discussions with my leadership team, we agreed that it would be valuable to have a written document that served as the foundation for all client-relationship decisions and put forth the guidelines for how those decisions would be made. A written document would eliminate any doubt about the importance of values to the enterprise.

With that in mind, we wrote the firm's client guideline, which we titled *Clients, Controversy and Difficult Decisions*. In truth, this document was simply an echo of what the founder of Burson-Marsteller, Harold Burson, has said over and over again for decades: "Integrity and respect have always formed the basis on which our firm is built."

This guideline had some basic assumptions, which I share in the spirit that everyone with character and values relies on similar core principles when they make important decisions.

- You are committed to protecting the reputation and integrity of the company you work for, your coworkers, and your clients.

- You always want to be proud of what you do. Likewise, you want to act in a way that makes everyone proud to be associated with you.

- You know that sometimes decisions that come down to your core values are not always clear-cut.

▮ The ultimate responsibility for your business relationships rests with you.

As you write your own values statement, I suggest you incorporate three critical components:

1. *A Focus on Lasting Values.* Values and proper ethical and moral behavior are at the core of business and the root of deciding what to do, say, and how to behave.

2. *Respect for Colleagues and Their Individual Viewpoints.* Respect for the integrity of the people around you means you would never encourage or even imply that anyone should compromise his/her own values by working on assignments that are not in accord with their values or beliefs. Similarly, you do not want to work in situations that would embarrass or otherwise compromise you.

3. *Responsibility for the Health of Your Career.* It is your responsibility to assess your career by asking a fundamental business question: In the long run, can you do what is being asked of you, and how will doing it affect your reputation?

Now . . . write your own. Declare your values in a way that is highly motivating and that you can return to again and again throughout your career. It will contribute to the power of your reputation because these values are true to who you are. This authenticity, discussed in depth in the next chapter, is vital to grounding your reputation in what is real.

chapter 4

Authenticity Rules

If you aren't yourself—if you aren't genuine—your team and your clients will figure it out. And, when that happens, there isn't anyone who's going to be buying what you're selling. Keep it honest. Keep it real. Remember, people make judgments about your character and your values. People aren't stupid.

—Bill Kearns, chairman of Keefe Ventures

WHILE WRITERS DRAFT speech material for executives, politicians, and presidents, the speaker often jumps in to change material at the last minute. The final notes—perhaps edited on the way to the meeting or the event—are filled with their handwritten changes. While the writers' core remarks may well have been terrific, these changes are even better.

Why? Because they are most often personal additions that reflect the heart of the person giving the speech. The result of these authentic additions is that he or she radiates the confidence of personal experience. And those who are listening feel it.

I remember having written a speech for a very talented chief executive in the entertainment business. He was receiving an award from a youth organization and wanted to encourage youngsters to try to do better than those who preceded them. The speech I wrote was titled "The Sons and Daughters of Evel Knievel." The message was simple: like the second-generation motorcycle daredevil Robbie Knievel, they too could outperform and outjump their dads' greatest accomplishments. Even though that speech remained mostly intact, during lunch the chief executive sat and slashed out paragraphs and inserted his own personal stories. Because he was speaking to a youth group, he wanted to talk about his own personal challenges as an orphan and tell how he accomplished what he did because of his perseverance and determination. This was the first time he had shared these struggles publicly, and the words he inserted conveyed both the struggle and the pride.

No one else could have written those words. Every good writer knows that it is those words that become the jewels of great communication and great reputations.

This was personal. This was genuine. This was powerful. The speech moved him and it moved others. It was written from a deep sense of confidence in why he did what he did throughout his life, day by day, in order to better himself and those around him. This was authentic. And it started with his very own confidence in how he felt and what he believed.

He encouraged the teenagers in the group to do the very same that he had, and these closing words were met with continuous applause and tears. It was the personal nature of the speech that gave it that much power. And the audience's receptivity and rousing response reaffirmed to the chief executive that who he truly is can be hugely appreciated.

Your Confidence Inspires Confidence in You

How you come across is vital to your reputation. To gain a good reputation that is based in reality, you must be genuine and clear, strong in your values, and stand up to scrutiny. You must be authentic . . . authentic in your ideas, your excitement, your enthusiasm, your pride, and your ability to share thoughts that are relevant to those with whom you meet and speak.

This link between authenticity and self-confidence—the courage to be who you truly are—is to be cherished, simply because it is real and it motivates.

When it comes to being perceived well and trusted, the strength of your own sense of confidence plays a critical role. If you are sure about what you believe and how you should behave, then others notice and are willing to follow. They see it as being genuine. Your sense of authentic confidence is contagious. They see it in your face. They can tell by the way you talk. There is an energy and a determination that those around you sense and *feel*. That *feeling* is the effect of confidence. You believe in yourself. You are ready. And others trust that. When they do, just about anything becomes possible.

This confidence is rooted in your sense of conviction that something is possible. Just read what Charles Lindbergh wrote about this kind of feeling, which he experienced as he sat in the cockpit of the *Spirit of St. Louis* at dawn on May 20, 1927. This is how he summoned the strength to open the throttle, pull the yoke, and take off for the first solo flight across the Atlantic, from New York to Paris.

> Wind, weather, power load—gradually those elements stop churning in my mind. It's less a decision of logic than of feeling, the kind of feeling that comes when you gauge the distance to be jumped between two stones across a brook. Something within you disengages itself from your body and travels ahead with your vision to make the test. You can feel it try the jump as you stand looking. Then uncertainty gives way to the conviction that it can or can't be done. Sitting in the cockpit, in seconds, minutes long, the conviction surges through me that the wheel will leave the ground, that the wings will rise above the wires, that it is time to start the flight.
>
> I buckle my safety belt, pull goggles down over my eyes, turn to the men at the blocks, and nod. Frozen figures leap to action. A yank on the ropes—the wheels are set free. I brace myself against the left side of the cockpit, sight along the edge of the runway, and ease the throttle wide open. Now, in seconds, we'll have the answer. Action brings confidence and relief.[1]

When you just know, inside, "that the wheel will leave the ground, that the wings will rise above the wires," others will sense your conviction and join you in your adventure—even if it's something no one has done before.

Through your life, I'm sure you've been tested. Whether you found yourself standing up for your values or your dreams, that experience helped you get to know what is important to you and who you are. Confidence is both the foundation and result of authenticity. It makes you strong enough to pursue what's important, and it is what you feel when you can be yourself completely.

Gaining an authentic reputation based on who you are can be effortless, as natural as breathing. At the same time, there are ways to establish this reputation intentionally so that people become a supportive part your talents, skills, visions, and goals. The rest of this chapter shares these simple ways we can express ourselves authentically.

Be Personal

One thing is for sure: there really isn't any distinction between our personal and our professional reputations. Other than traveling back and forth to an office, plant, or store each day for work, it's sometimes hard to know where one begins and the other leaves off. That, actually, is a strength and a positive thing. It makes your actions and your reputation even more genuine because you don't cross borderlines between aspects of your life. Your sense of values, ethics, respect for others, caring, honesty, courage, and integrity . . . all of your traits are visible regardless of where you are at any given moment. This helps people get to know you, the whole you, which is the true art of establishing a reputation.

So why shouldn't we be more open about what and who we are when we are at work? Some people just can't. They feel that they have to be guarded. Depending on whom you work with and your organization's culture, that could be the best—or perhaps a wisely conservative—path to take. But in most cases, people will enjoy getting to know you better. They will enjoy having something else to talk about other than the spreadsheet you're working on together.

Bring Your Interests to Work

I hope you have the good fortune to help shape the culture of the organization where you work. Whether you are a small-business owner, a high-ranking corporate executive, the manager of a satellite office, an office manager, or the person in charge of staff events, you can do things that are quite different and often even original. Those initiatives tell more about your character and your personality than otherwise might have been possible.

Here are a few examples of the ways I have brought who I am to work. Something similar might also work for you.

▮ Whenever I make a speech—within the firm or to outside groups—there is always something personal in the message. It might be a reference to my children, my family, or my upbringing. Or it is a quote from a favorite author, the view of an historian that has relevance today, a personal story about the challenges of doing what is needed—even when it is tough—an event from my life that helped shape my views or my expectations of others. I've found without fail that this addition imbues the power of authenticity into the rest of the speech.

▮ When the baseball World Series gets under way each year, I walk through the office and distribute either National League or American League baseballs to the entire staff. Yes, I am a big-time baseball fan, but personally handing out those balls has more to do with office camaraderie and spirit than with those seven ball games.

▮ Each year, on the evening before the first day of spring, I arranged to have small, individual bouquets of daffodils delivered to the desk of each member of my staff. That way, the next morning when they arrived, there were blossoms of yellow at each desk to greet them. Flowers in bloom say a lot about spirit, expectation, and promise. Plus, there is nothing like flowers to put a smile on everyone's face.

▮ I have always loved art. On the top floor of our building, there was a rather large open space. Long before I ever arrived at the firm, it had been called the Gallery. I thought we should use it as an actual gallery to showcase our own staff's creativity. In the public relations and advertising business, there are many extraordinarily talented and creative people. So I asked myself, Why not display their creations? We did just that. And within a few weeks, the Gallery was filled with drawings, paintings, sculpture, photographs, macramé, CD covers, lyrics, videos, and music scores sent in by countless numbers of people from our offices throughout the world. So many others clamored to send in their artwork that we could change the Gallery exhibition on a regular basis. We gave exposure to the artistic pursuits of our staff and they basked in the limelight. You could see the pride and joy whenever members of our staff showed their colleagues what they had created, now on display. Never had that happened to them before.

❙ For each meeting of my executive board—my immediate direct reports—I brought in a book to give to the board members. The book might be about our business or it might simply be a book that I treasured or simply read but thought would be interesting to others. This gesture was meant to say something about our business being an intellectual one, in which learning was a day-to-day goal.

Many of those things were fun. But none of them were just for fun. Rather, they spoke about culture, character, values, respect for, and appreciation of hard work. They were also contributions to the culture that I felt I could personally give.

Your personal character is a powerful driver of success. Do what you can to bring who you are to work and to involve others in your passions in ways that make them shine. This will definitely get your name circulated around the office, and a reputation will form based on the interests you bring. Plus, what you do and what you show of yourself create a loud voice to proclaim how important every individual is to long-term success. As we'll talk about later in the book, supporting others in their success is a sure way to a great reputation.

Foster a Culture of Openness

Management schools will be the first to teach you that if there are contentious professional relationships within a company, that organization is usually fraught with problems, insurmountable conflict, divisive politics, and lack of productivity. Success often eludes those organizations. They may even wither and die, sometimes slowly and other times quite quickly. For our success and the success of our enterprise, we need to build a base of trust in our working relationships. This leads to a culture of openness.

Those who work with you are very perceptive. They can tell if you are pretending, putting on airs, or not being genuine. If you are down to earth and treat the people you work with honestly, they will stay on your side to the ends of the earth.

In short, authenticity and trust go hand-in-hand.

If those around you see your authentic qualities, they will trust you and be more eager to participate and less hesitant about sharing their views. That, in turn, creates discussions and constructive engagement on issues that are substantive, unpretentious, and open to collaboration. Exciting things can happen because that same openness brings to the surface new and sometimes revolutionary ideas that may otherwise have been lost in a less open, less trusting culture.

Most successful organizations thrive on the exchange of ideas. In that process, the idea is tested through debate, and shaped by others. The toughest questions produce the strongest ideas, initiatives, and inventions. If you want to thrive, open up and show your true colors. Others will reciprocate and the entire organization will benefit.

Authentic Action

People can get to know you by what you say and what you do. If the two go hand-in-hand, they will see your authenticity and confidence play out in your day-to-day activity.

In the moment before you act, whether you realize it at the time or not, you make a decision regarding *how* to act. Even relatively minor decisions about how to approach a given situation can pave the way as stepping-stones for major successes or failures. Conversely, what might otherwise seem to be major decisions sometimes prove to be not all that important in the long run. The fact is that you may never really know at the outset.

This quality of not knowing brings importance to every decision about how to act. Each decision needs to be viewed through a prism of character, values, and authenticity.

As you move through positions of greater and greater responsibility in your career, build a systematic thought process or a series of questions that you always ask yourself when faced with making a decision to act in some way. Think of it as an exercise or a series of *proof points* that you demand of yourself at every stage. As a starter, ask yourself these questions. Then, as you become more familiar with your own process, you can design your own questions to pose.

▎What is the magnitude of the decision, and how will my actions affect others?

❙ What does my decision say about me and my values?

❙ Is my decision in keeping with what I am like as a person? Is it an authentic statement by me?

❙ If I am pressed to explain, what would I say is the underlying value or principle on which I built my decision?

❙ Will my decision stand the test of time?

❙ Am I proud of my decision?

When deciding what you will do, what you will say, and how you will speak, you should view those actions through a lens that can anticipate and interpret how others are likely to react. Consider their perspective as a part of your decision-making process. Simply put, everyone is watching you closely, and they will make judgments. Clearly, if you want to ensure your success, it then goes without saying that you should never do or say anything that contradicts the particular qualities and values that underscore the reputation you so desire and need.

If everyone is watching what you do and say, you cannot afford a misstep. You cannot afford a blow to your reputation—perceived or otherwise. Every step of the way, you must be seen to be genuine and your actions in keeping with your reputation. By asking yourself the questions posed in the following list, you can effectively put yourself in the shoes of the public and of individuals who are important to you.

❙ Would I be comfortable if my actions—my thought process and the final decision—were the subject of an article on the front page of the *Washington Post,* the *New York Times, The Financial Times,* or *The International Herald Tribune?*

❙ Could I comfortably respond to the late-night online bloggers if they were to criticize my actions?

❙ What if I had to testify before Congress, facing harsh questions and the bright glare of television cameras and high-intensity lights, answering the question of why I decided to do what I did?

❙ And more important, what if I had to explain to my son or daughter—mother or father—why I decided what I did?

These questions can be posed both hypothetically and realistically. Having these public and private spheres in mind effectively puts you in the shoes of reputation shapers. When considering our reputation, imagining the feedback we will get from important entities and people can draw attention to blind spots and make us consider a situation as we might not have otherwise done.

Don't Play Games

Phonies don't last. If you are not genuine, you will be found out. As Abraham Lincoln is reputed to have said: *You can fool some of the people all of the time, and all of the people some of the time, but you cannot fool all of the people all of the time.*

The fact is that people are not stupid. Think about the number of times when someone has talked to you, told you something, or tried to sell you something. What was your reaction? Did you believe that person? Did you instinctively trust him or her?

Your gut reaction was probably the best indicator to use. If that gut reaction told you that the person was handing you a line or not being entirely truthful, you probably picked it up. People perceive more than they might admit at first.

When it comes to your reputation, it is important to realize that if you aren't genuine—if you aren't authentic—people will figure you out. For example, don't try to fool people; be straight with them. Don't posture for power; it never works. Don't talk down to others, and don't pretend to be someone you aren't. Later in the book, in Chapter 7, I am going to discuss the temptation to use "spin" or to spin things in your favor. That, too, comes down to matters of authenticity and respect.

Landing Clients Authentically

Bill Kearns is chairman of Keefe Ventures, a money management firm, and a former managing director in corporate finance at Lehman Brothers when that firm was an industry leader, years before its troubles. He saw firsthand how strong working relationships were built, how they impact reputation, and how they paved the way for the future. His story of success is built on relating to clients authentically, which often made all the difference. In this interview, he offers some great tips for creating a genuine connection.

To me, it's all rather simple. What you do demonstrates your character. If you want to build relationships with people who work for you or those for whom you work, you have to do the things that are substantive and make a difference. Look them in the eye and tell them what is real. Don't fake it. Don't overpromise. Saying that you will do something means nothing less...get it done.

The guiding principles for how you need to behave are really simple. Some people overcomplicate them and, in the process, what is most important falls by the wayside.

Give them a firm handshake. And be ready to be tested. More than once, when it first looked like I had lost the opportunity to raise funds for my corporate clients, I got a second chance. The answer always was the same...that client had tried the other firm, they had promised but hadn't delivered at the original fee. The banker tried to raise the fee, and the client walked. Quite simple.

With time, reputation grew and business followed. I had always believed it was important to be seen as a person who would provide thoughtful and realistic advice. That meant research. It meant great staff work and preparation. It meant being direct, truthful, and straightforward...it meant working to win their trust.

And, of course, a little humor, humility, good nature, and candor were other important qualities in the mix. Tell a joke now and then. Remember those anecdotes that make people laugh. Why? Because, at the end of the day, we are all individuals and most of us would prefer to do business with those we like to be around. It's just human nature.

Sometimes that first handshake does make all the difference. Or the joke you tell to put a nervous person at ease or to relax a tense situation, oʄ the personal story you tell about one of your children to break the ice. People remember those personal touches, those things make them like yǫu. And that is a great basis for your reputation. Large organization or small, there really is little difference when it comes to developing strong, respectful, results-driven working relationships that are built on authentic character. Every relationship is important. Even if it doesn't appear so right now, you can be assured that it will in the future as people consider you to be the person they would do business with over someone else.

The Double-Edged Sword of the Digital World

Our rapidly growing digital world has dramatically changed not only the way that individuals and organizations communicate but also the way that reputations are built, questioned, or thrown into doubt.

Access to the Internet on laptops, touch pads, mobile devices, smartphones and other hand-held digital devices has made expressing thoughts and opinions—whether thought through or not—a quick and easy matter. Regardless of where someone is or the time of day or night, he or she can share thoughts about an event, an organization, or an individual. Researched and well founded or unfounded and biased, those comments and opinions travel around the world at mega speeds and are read by people who may have no frame of reference for what they are reading. You may never have met those who are writing about you or your organization—nor have they ever seen you—but you will feel the brunt of their comments.

The new universe of social networking sites, blogs, chats, viral messages and videos, texts, new media, e-blasts, and websites is rapidly expanding every day. This digital world can lead to new challenges, unforeseen opportunities, and new relationships. It can create product successes in record time, launch new initiatives, and create excitement about a innovative venture. At the same time, because of its power, it can also sway public opinion and swing elections or urge boycotts . . . even foster riots, demonstrations, and insurrections. If it can do that, think what it can do for or to your reputation.

It is a potent force today, both positive and negative.

How about those pictures posted on Facebook? Those chat or text comments by someone who has never even met you or, worse yet, you thought knew you well or cared about you? Or those stories told by nameless individuals as they blogged well into the night?

In the world of hard drives and Internet postings, words and images last forever, unlike the days of yesterday when paper was shredded and documents erased.

This new technology has put an even higher premium on strong reputations and authenticity. And it has put a stronger emphasis on what you do every day in this online world to shape that reputation in the way you want, starting at the earliest moments of your career, from the smallest steps you take to the biggest decisions you make.

Selling Authentically

Whether you are a fundraiser or a salesperson selling products and services, genuinely believing in what you have to offer is the most powerful way to close a deal. Rose Mann is assistant dean of advancement for the Rosenstiel School of Marine and Atmospheric Science at the University of Miami. With its roots dating to the 1940s, the Rosenstiel School is likely the world's leading marine and atmospheric research institution. The campus on Virginia Key houses its research facilities and the dock for its research vessel, which is used to study fish, migratory patterns, and marine species—all with the goal of preserving marine life. Rose's story offers clear advice based on what she has learned in convincing donors of the merits of her institution.

> My job is to raise funds for the school and we are well on our way to being able to build a completely new research facility. This kind of funding through donations could never have been possible if so many wonderful people weren't ready and willing to give to Rosenstiel. They don't give because they have to. They have plenty of other choices. But these are individuals who have come to respect the school, what we stand for, and they have confidence in how we will use their money.
>
> This kind of reputation is priceless. Ours is one of those cases where perception and reality are exactly the same. That applies to the University of Miami, to the Rosenstiel School, to the dean here, and to me. They know [that] the kind of research done by Rosenstiel to

help save the oceans is important. For me, this quest is also part of my life. When I talk to potential donors, they can sense that. I speak with conviction, simply because it is true. I have lived and worked near the ocean my entire life. I have seen its potential and I have seen some of the disasters that have affected marine life, right here in the Atlantic, the Caribbean, and the Gulf.

I might be a fundraiser but I don't sell. In fact, I don't know how to sell. I can't sell. What I can do is speak from the heart about something that is so vital to me and others. I can't encourage someone to give if it doesn't mean something to me. I believe in it. I simply tell the truth. Of course, I have to be knowledgeable or else I have little of substance to add. But I love this school and what we do. And it shows.

I manage a staff each of whom has the same commitment as I and, without them, none of what we do would be possible. All of them feel the passion. They have to. It is part of the group's culture. Our prospective donors must hear and feel the excitement. And there cannot be any disconnect between perception and reality.

People build their perceptions of others on a very personal level. They might see me as an extension of the school but, when we start to talk, they are looking at a person. Based on what they sense, they will decide to trust. They make judgments about me. And, if they believe I am genuine and committed, they will act accordingly.

When that happens more than once, a reputation emerges. And other people echo that trust. It's that simple.

As Mann points out, everyone can feel your enthusiasm. Research what you're selling to the point at which you believe there is nothing better out there, and be knowledgeable about the competition. When you are thoroughly convinced of the good your product or service does, as Mann says, "perception and reality are exactly the same." This is the most powerful place from which to sell anything.

In Chapter 7, you will gain some vital tips for sharing your knowledge and enthusiasm with others.

Transparency and Authenticity Drive Trust

We are in an era in which the demand for candor, understanding, and clarity of purpose is greater than ever before. Transparency creates confidence and underscores authenticity. In turn, they create a climate of trust in which businesses are better likely to deliver results and careers better able to be successful.

Investors demand transparency in financial disclosure by chief executives and financial officers. Patients want transparency from those in the health-care field so they know more about treatment options. And employees want transparency in goals and objectives from all those with whom they work.

Transparency in business is the framework for authenticity. The two go hand-in-hand. And trust follows.

If you aren't transparent, then you aren't authentic. You are hiding something. There is something you don't want to share . . . or perhaps you are afraid of sharing. Regardless, it affects those with whom you work and detracts from your ability to project the right motives and build success. And people are less likely to trust.

Character—seen as authentic—and transparency of actions are paramount to a strong reputation and a successful career.

As our kids say, "Keep it real."

A Genuine Legacy

As Thomas Jefferson wrote in his letter of January 12, 1819, to Nathaniel Macon, U.S. senator and revolutionary war soldier:

> Whether the succeeding generation is to be more virtuous than their predecessors, I cannot say; but I am sure they will have more worldly wisdom, and enough, I hope, to know that honesty is the first chapter in the book of wisdom.

As we make our business decisions and act on them, as we solicit business and build our careers, we need to reflect on the generational legacy we are leaving. Thinking ahead to the legacy you are leaving is a sign of personal character. If we can leave our kids something real, we will leave our kids a world rooted in genuine caring. Just because you are one person, don't think you can't influence the world for the better. Your reputation can extend your values into a workplace environment and make waves that impact the future. That is why, after we have learned about establishing what we stand for and developing the courage to be authentic, a chapter on caring and respect for others naturally follows.

NOTE

1. Charles A. Lindbergh, *The Spirit of St. Louis* (New York: Scribner, 1953), p. 185.

chapter 5

Caring and Respect

I've learned you never know who might be a donor. It might be the entrepreneur or the fisherman. Or the boat builder. Or it might be the janitor. The lesson for me is that you treat everyone with respect and kindness.

—Rose Mann, assistant dean of advancement
for the Rosenstiel School of Marine and
Atmospheric Science at the University of Miami

THROUGHOUT MY CAREER, whenever I changed jobs, I devoted at least the entire first day of my new job to walking every floor of the building. I started in the basement—from storage, to production, to the mailroom, and then on to the next floor until I reached the executive offices at the top. At each office and workspace, I stopped, shook every employee's hand, and we talked for a few moments. We seldom talked about work. Rather, we talked about family, whether they liked their job, and why.

That walk took hours. Yet I learned more about the people and they learned more about me than would have otherwise been possible. Plus, their first introduction to me was done in a very personal way...no pretense, no false preparation, no formality. It was simply two professionals meeting for the first time. It was also on their turf...not mine.

As I moved from floor to floor, I had a growing sense about the office's personality, and employees began to develop their own "feeling" about me. At this stage, a common bond first began to form. There was no reason not to trust one another. And we were on the same page.

Even after I was well into my new duties, I tried to walk the halls once a month so that I could personally say hello to as many as were in the office that day, ask about them, and how they were doing.

Why did I do this? Because it is commonly known to be a good strategy? No—I did it because I cared. I wanted to start off knowing who people were and what was important to them.

Claude Ritman made hospitals his career. By the time he turned 50, he was named executive director of Coler-Goldwater Hospital in New York City.

> There is little more effective than "walking the halls." There are 2,000 beds at Coler-Goldwater, on two campuses. While no one can visit each patient every week and still do their job, you have to make a point of making the rounds, just like the doctors.

Create an Envelope of Caring

Let the people you work with know you care about each of them and their careers. When you walk around the workplace, visit a client's office, or stop by a vendor's warehouse, stop and talk to people as individuals. This is important whether you are a CEO or an administrator—if people see your face and your smile, if you ask how they are, that contributes to an environment of caring. After all, they all have personal lives . . . families, children, friends, and hobbies. Showing a sincere interest in them and a sense of caring generates the warmth of friendship and a bond that makes them think well of you, speak well of you, and look after your well-being. This is a sure recipe for a good reputation.

In his acclaimed book *The Speed of Trust: The One Thing That Changes Everything*, Stephen M.R. Covey wrote:

> In the dictionary, intent is defined as "plan" or "purpose." I am convinced that no discussion of intent would be complete without talking about three things: motive, agenda, and behavior.

Motive. The motive that inspires the greatest trust is genuine caring—caring about people, caring about purposes, caring about the quality of what you do, caring about society as a whole.

The trust we have in people and in organizations comes, in part, from believing that they do care.

Agenda. Agenda grows out of motive. It's what you intend to do or promote because of your motive.

The agenda that generally inspires the greatest trust is seeking mutual benefit—genuinely wanting what's best for everyone involved.

Behavior. Typically, behavior is the manifestation of motive and agenda. The behavior that best creates credibility and inspires trust is acting in the best interests of others. When we do so, we clearly demonstrate the intent of caring and the agenda of seeking mutual benefit. And this is where the rubber meets the road. It's easy to say "I care" and "I want you to win," but it is our actual behavior that demonstrates whether or not we mean it.[1]

Clearly, to Covey the most important factor in building trust is caring and acting with everyone's welfare in mind. Caring for others is a value that is as much at the core of who we are as is our sense of honesty. It is as human as parenthood. And it can even be a more powerful motivating factor than money.

Build Your Reputation with Caring and Sharing

One of the most critical tasks of people who want to be successful in their careers is to make the people they work with feel wanted and valued. Just ask Dr. Phil McGraw. In a broadcast segment that looked at relationships and what it takes to make them healthy and productive, Dr. Phil concluded with some pointed advice that is as important for our careers as it is in other areas of our lives.

You know, I think a good rule to embrace is that you deal with people, whoever—waiter, spouse, brother, sister, friend—you deal with them in a way that protects or enhances their self-esteem. Because, I'll promise you, if you engage people in a way that whenever you finish that interaction with them, they feel better about themselves than they did before they encountered you, you're going to be a success.[2]

Caring is extraordinarily important and essential for the kind of reputation that endures and builds a framework for success. If you don't demonstrate that you care, you will not be followed. More important, you will not be trusted.

The challenge is that the concept of caring is difficult to describe, let alone difficult for some even to accept. In the business world, particularly, it often is misinterpreted as a weakness. In the nonprofit or charity world, it is just the opposite. It is recognized as a key asset. In some cases, people go so far as to view "toughness" as the alternative to caring.

I look at this no differently than I look at the concept of sharing authority and responsibility. Here too, people equate sharing or giving up some power as a weakness. On the surface it might seem that way. But sharing, like caring, is a sign of partnership and trust. It is the most dramatic form of telling a person with whom you work that you are willing to cast your fate along with him or her.

As chief executive of a counseling firm, my philosophy was simple: I wanted to partner with as many people as possible, my caring being a signal that I was as vested in their futures as I expected them to be in mine. I wanted to share both the glory and the agony, because I believed that together we could do more than I could alone. It is the simple concept that as we grow in an organization, any organization, we need others to help us succeed. And to get their support, we need to care about their futures, partner with them, and share the success. That makes them feel good about themselves and the important roles you have asked them to play. Their self-esteem grows. Their confidence builds. And they outperform.

In turn, they feel loyalty and feel good about you. The combination is a winning one.

And, ultimately, if you care and share power, you will get more power in return because others will follow and support you.

The same thing holds true regardless of your job. The fact is that caring and sharing empower others to do their best. They become vested in their own performance because you have reached out to them and you trust them to be your partners. That single act demonstrates the importance of their role and solidifies their loyalty.

Celia Berk, chief talent officer for Young & Rubicam Group, talks about how she does this.

> I start from a base of respect for the individual. If they come to me with a problem, I need to understand their thought process. I want to relate to them on a personal basis because it gives me the opportunity to really hear what they are saying.

This holds true whether you are looking to win clients, expand a customer base, or establish a business partnership. Inclusion means everything when it comes to building a reputation that works.

Make no mistake. Caring and sharing are not signs of weakness. They are signs of strength and they help you develop the best framework for thinking strategically, building operational plans, reaching financial and business goals, setting measurable objectives, and holding yourself and others accountable. They do not take away from the discipline necessary to run a successful organization and produce a bottom line that is at or above industry standards. And they do not undermine any sense of strong leadership.

Caring and sharing are building blocks for reputation, character, and a feeling among everyone you do business with that what you are doing is special, fueled by respect, sharing power and responsibility, and caring for each other.

There are seven steps to successful caring and sharing:

1. Pick the people you work with well—focus on those whom you trust explicitly.

2. Vest them with the raw facts —be candid and make sure they are aware of all the potential problems, the risks, and the challenges.

3. Don't oversell their roles or the opportunities—make sure they understand how difficult the challenges are.

4. Let them talk—use any discussions with them as a means of engagement in looking for solutions. Keep every discussion a dialog.

5. Ask them if they need help—then help them get the resources they need.

6. Check in to see how they are doing—don't check on them but check in with them.

7. Share the victory and the failures—if you chose your team well, then be confident . . . they can handle the good, the bad, and the ugly.

Respect Individual Viewpoints

Successful people develop trust by respecting everyone's views. If those who work with you believe in you and know you respect each one of them and their views, they will return that respect. They will place more value and trust in your decisions, listen more attentively to your reasons, and work that much harder to accomplish the task at hand. Most times, they will follow more eagerly and approach assignments or goals with greater resolve and commitment.

Some may see this as daunting, but it actually is simpler to do than many may think. The starting point is key: you must approach your relationship with colleagues, clients, and team members with the attitude that they have a great deal to offer and that their views may make the difference between success and failure.

If those with whom you work know you genuinely want their ideas, they will measure up to the task. But it is your job to convince them that you are genuine and that they will be seen as partners. And that starts right at the beginning.

Here are some points to make when you speak to the people you work with:

❙ We have an opportunity to make a difference.

❙ Making a difference will only happen with us working as a team, personally devoted to the best we can do.

I I want your ideas. I want the good ones and the ones you might not think are so good. And those that others have said won't work.

I Don't be afraid to speak up.

I Challenge me.

I Don't let me hand you any sort of excuse, such as "been tried before but didn't work."

I If you genuinely believe in your idea, your strategy, or your initiative, fight for it.

I Nothing good comes without overcoming hurdles.

I Nothing great comes without risk.

I Nothing extraordinary comes without sacrifice.

I This is personal for me and I want it to be personal for you. If it is, we will accomplish more.

I believe that in life you get what you give. If you are open to new ideas, you will get new ideas. If you are appreciative of others, they will appreciate you and what you do for them. If you show your respect for other views, those people will be quicker to respect yours. And if you care about them, they will care about you. When that happens, everyone wins.

Treat Everyone as Partners and Equals

Treat everyone with the dignity and with the respect they deserve. They each have something to offer and will make the greatest contribution to your endeavor if they know you trust them, expect them to perform at their best, value their input, and are giving them opportunities that stretch their abilities. You may be surprised by those you least expect.

As the most senior leader of a business, I believed that my key partners were my global chief financial officer and my global human resource/talent officer. The three of us were a team. My reasoning was simple: people—our talent—and our financial performance were key drivers of success. I was the operational executive and the final decision maker, but I couldn't do my job without them.

Did some people wonder why I would give up what seemed like some of my power in order to closely engage two key executives as partners in the future of the business? Yes. Did they wonder why I was taking this kind of position about caring and sharing? Yes. But I was only questioned by those who followed an outdated form of management, in which power and authority are concentrated in one person. History shows that style to be unsuccessful in the long run.

The critical issue is your own genuine attitude. The question is this: Do you come across as a person who cares and genuinely wants to hear what others have to say or are you just giving them lip service?

Lead by Caring

Jack Welch, retired chairman and chief executive of General Electric (GE), who held those positions for a remarkable twenty years, focused directly on this issue in his bestselling book, *Winning*. In contrast to his public image of being so very tough, his real message is crystal clear:

> Before you are a leader, success is all about yourself.
>
> When you become a leader, success is all about growing others.
>
> Take every opportunity to inject self-confidence into those who have earned it.
>
> Use ample praise, the more specific the better.[3]

When Jack Welch talks about helping others, he is speaking directly to the importance of caring about those with whom you work. He doesn't mean that you interject yourself into their personal lives, even though you may often reach out and ask how someone is doing. Nor is he only thinking about praise and kind words.

This is not soft stuff. It is the heart of any relationship and especially those that encourage individuals to do their very best. If you manage a staff, whether one person, a department, or a whole company, if you manage from a place of caring and respect, people will respond. Steve Joenk, president and CEO of AXA Equitable Funds Management

Group, LLC, provides a good example of this in sharing his management approach:

> I love what Maya Angelou once said: "I've learned that people will forget what you said, people will forget what you did, but people will never forget how you made them feel."
>
> I wish that kind of "constructive and supportive feeling" for all those who work with me because one of the most important functions managers can perform is to mentor others so that they can, in turn, be effective managers. I consider that my job. One of the best things we can do is provide opportunities for others. And part of helping people to take advantage of those opportunities is for them to not be afraid of reaching out and seeing how much they can accomplish. For that to happen, they need to be at ease and comfortable. If I am trusted and behave in a manner that demonstrates trust for others, then it will work. And that feeling will be there.
>
> If I respect others and they see that I do, then they will be more enthusiastic and motivated in how they undertake their own responsibilities.

Looking for Heart

When the time comes to make changes in a business, you reach out and look for talent and heart. Of course talent . . . that goes without saying. You need professional expertise to grow and build the business. You need managers and leaders who know how to make strategic and operational decisions and do them in a decisive way.

But heart? That's different. Who needs heart, caring, and respect when you're in the trenches, working to move things in a new direction?

We all do.

At one point in my career when I was looking to name a new president for our U.S. operations, I asked one of our senior executives, Chet Burchett, to meet me for dinner on a Sunday evening. I knew him well and had asked him to fly in from Chicago that morning. With a great track record in our industry and a personal reputation to match, I knew the credentials were there. But we came from very different backgrounds so it was important to spend time comparing notes about priorities and how we dealt with people. We chatted for a while about our values, especially what was important to us in building a business in which our teams were motivated to do the very best. Good was good. Everyone knows that. But great was the goal. At the firm, we had taken the bold step to define our business as being "the gold standard" in the industry. For that to be real, just good wasn't good enough.

By the time the dinner ended, I knew that Chet was the right person to take charge of our largest operation. He was eager for the challenge, and it was clear that he was ready to start. You could tell by his enthusiasm that his energy and caring would be infectious.

Chet was a midwesterner at heart. He had spent much of his life and working career in Chicago and the surrounding states. In the style of so many talented people from the Midwest, he, too, "wore his heart on his sleeve."

I love that. It means that a person shows emotion . . . you show how you feel. You care. But it doesn't mean that you get carried away or burst into a tirade and lose control. Not at all.

Rather, it means that you care and that you share your feelings with those around you. And with that caring comes respect for others because you take the time to understand what motivates them. When you care, others care. When you respect others, they respect in return. And when you ask them to reach new heights, they do just that.

That was Chet. It was how he was seen by others. It was integral to his reputation. He always spoke from the heart. When he knew a decision was right, not only did he talk in clear, straightforward terms about the cold, hard business rationale, but he could also share how strongly he felt about what steps everyone had to take to make it a success. You knew that he would be first in line to do the tough jobs. And you knew that he would be last in line to get the credit.

Chet reached people in very personal ways. He often spoke about the quality of the work we did. When he did, he cautioned about accepting second best. He would refer to the social scientist theory that broken windows lead to decay in urban environments, using the theory as a warning that even the smallest lapse in quality standards could lead to a decline in the overall quality of the work we did. After September 11, 2001, he wrote often with great feeling to his team and started to use the phrase "the new normal" to help keep them motivated after the tragedy. And he was part of the firm's global leadership team when we were named Large PR Agency of the Year by the industry's leading publication.

The Art of Caring

Caring needs to be viewed as a genuine outreach to make sure that those who work with you have both the guidance and encouragement to do their best. If you want to motivate people in the work environment, you first need to know enough about an individual's strength and weaknesses so that you can provide the purposeful kind of resources that help both the person and the organization to succeed.

Accomplishing that starts with devoting the energy so that you do understand what makes people tick and you do understand what will motivate them. Your involvement with them makes them feel good about themselves—good about their potential to do great things and good about what they can contribute. It builds self-confidence.

So how to do that?

Start by spending time with people and listening to what they have to say. Learn from them. When they talk, they will tell you as much about themselves as they do about their ideas. Talk to them as if you are talking to a customer. Ask them what is important and what they would recommend. Don't jump in. Just listen. That is the key step to engaging them for the long run. If they believe you want to know, they will know you care.

By reaching out to others, you send important signals about yourself and you build a reputation as someone to whom others look for motivation. They come to expect you to listen and motivate.

Encouragement can take many forms. Sometimes it is as simple as encouraging others to apply their insights and skills. I remember being part of a team that was meeting a Fortune 100 company for the first time to talk about working for them. We all flew to Los Angeles the night before and agreed to meet in one of the hotel rooms at 8:00 the next morning to review our presentation, which was scheduled for just after lunch. When we sat down to review the presentation "deck," it was clear that it had been put together by different people and it lacked clarity and a consistent style. One of the team members—a junior staff person who was relatively new to the firm—started to share her ideas on how it should be changed. A discussion ensued and different viewpoints were shared. Some of the more senior people, perhaps protective of the existing presentation because they helped in its construction, were dismissive of her ideas.

An extraordinary thing happened when the team leader looked at the junior staffer and told her to take the deck and rework it so that it had clarity and a unifying style. Everyone else was startled. And, for sure, the junior staffer was apprehensive.

But the team leader was experienced. He had made a point of talking to her on the plane the previous day and he had a sense of what she could do. So, he took a chance. Two hours later, the team regrouped to review the revised presentation. Was it perfect? No. But the logic was clear, the ideas were dynamic, and there was an intellectual thread that wove through the document, making the recommendations clear and concise.

Who won the most in that exchange? The junior staffer and the team leader. Not because the team won the business, but because caring and trust emerged like never before. The team was energized, the junior staffer was thrilled, and the team leader reinforced a reputation of caring, sharing, and encouraging others.

Caring About Customers

If you own a business, perhaps you started it because you saw a gap in the marketplace and you knew you could fill it. Perhaps you developed a skill, expertise, or product that few others could offer. Whatever the case, if you build your business around caring for your clients in the best way possible, you will earn a reputation that will earn repeat business and will attract more through word of mouth—which is the most powerful form of advertising you can get.

Manny and Lily Dominguez have built their independently owned family business around caring about their patients' needs. Here's how they do it.

> I call everyone who comes into my pharmacy my patient. I treat them that way . . . not as customers but as patients. I know that I can't just fill the prescription. If I am to continue to be successful, I have to do more. I must understand customers and do all I can to satisfy them. I must know any other medications they take. Some -

times, I talk with the physician. I also know that there are times when the patient can't pay right then but can pay when their next check arrives. If they are on Social Security, Medicare, or on a pension, there are times when I have to be flexible. Since the two of us share the manager job—we are the bosses—we make those decisions.

The pharmacy becomes an extension of our values and our beliefs.

Our patients feel that they are going to someone they know. They know us as a couple. We are there for them. We are an extension of their family. For us, that is critical. Some might call it old-fashioned but we think it has created a very special reputation for us and that has been crucial to our success. At the end of the day, word of mouth matters most. Our success is hinged on a reputation that encourages patients to want to talk to us and feel that we provide what they need. That is a very special relationship—special to how others see us.

You know, it's really pretty simple. No matter who you are, when you're sick, you're sick. And we are here to listen and help.

If clients believe you are there for them, that you understand their specific needs and address them in your product or service, your success will radiate through the most precious form of advertising—word of mouth. But this takes genuine caring.

The next part of this book looks at the ways you can demonstrate your personal character, values, authenticity, and caring by communicating them in all you say and do. After all, it is our actions that mean the most. And when they reflect what we hold most dear, we gain the trust that underlies a good reputation.

NOTES

1. Stephen M. R. Covey, *The Speed of Trust: The One Thing That Changes Everything* (New York: Free Press, 2006), pp. 78–81.

2. Dr. Phil, December 27, 2010, Harpo Inc. Reprinted with permission.

3. Jack Welch, *Winning* (New York: HarperCollins, 2005), pp. 66, 70, 71, 78, 79.

part two

communication

The automatic trust is not there. Society says, "Show me," "Be transparent," and "Why should I believe you?" The world is much more critical. And if you go from this "trust me" to this "show me" world, then it is very important that the senior leaders are very good communicators.

—Jeroen van der Veer, retired CEO of Royal Dutch Shell,
in an interview published by *McKinsey Quarterly*, July 2009[1]

History has shown that we never know exactly when our actions and our words—our reputation—will be put under the microscope. But it will come. We will be tested, perhaps even more than once.

What we know for sure is that the microscope has a powerful lens. How we behave, in both expected and unexpected situations, is very closely watched. When it comes to communicating who we are as a businessperson and when the moment of our greatest challenge arrives, our responses must be firmly grounded in authentic character. This is how true communication happens, the kind that shapes perception and reputation. This is how we show people we truly care.

The area at the southern tip of Manhattan where the twin World Trade Towers once stood has long now been called Ground Zero. For all of us, especially those who were living or working in New York City on September 11, 2001, it was a day that we will never forget. Nor will we forget the weeks that followed. The tragedy was of untold proportion. It destroyed a great number of lives and changed others forever.

Our office building was at 19th Street and Park Avenue South. From the elevator lobby on the top floor, the window looked due south. I arrived in the building that Tuesday morning at my usual time, around six o'clock. The weather was spectacular, the sky a bright blue. When I got off the elevator and looked out that window, it was as if I could see forever. The twin towers stood in the distance against a clear sky.

I went into my office, turned on the television as I usually did, and went about the day. At 8:46, the first plane crashed into the North Tower. I heard the news and saw the photos broadcast on CNN. Like so many others who were now in the office, I went to the elevator lobby to look out the window. At 9:03, those still in the lobby saw what we thought was the second plane crash into the South Tower. You couldn't help but cry out in shock. And people cried when they saw what happened. A short while later, those who were still in the lobby actually saw the Towers collapse.

As the most senior manager in the firm, the next steps were mine. What should we do? This was not a predictable event nor one we could imagine having to prepare for.

We went into action and marshaled our resources to make sure that all of our people were accounted for and safe. From there, all our efforts went into communication. Through an office-wide meeting, regular updates, and by making human resources available to everyone who felt they wanted to talk, we made sure to tend to everyone's needs. And the best way to do that was to give everyone the chance to speak and be heard.

That afternoon, at 2:32, I sent the entire firm—2,000 people in offices around the world—an e-mail to let them know what we knew, what our reactions were, and how our colleagues throughout the world were reacting. I continued to send these updates over the next ten days.

In my e-mail to staff on September 12, headlined "Day Two of the Tragedy in New York and Washington," I wrote in part:

> The most extraordinary thing about people facing hardship is how resolve and strength surface. Our goal is to be strong and determined, help others and rebuild. Our hearts and prayers are with everyone—we've all been affected in some way.

The e-mail to staff on "Day Three" told of just that kind of resolve and strength:

> Even though there is much we still don't know and will not know for some time—especially details about the toll on human life—many of our colleagues have been leading the way by focusing their energies on things constructive and purposeful.
>
> This is absolutely the right thing to do. We will continue to be horrified by this terrible act but strength and recovery mean "taking action . . . purposeful action."
>
> Inside the company, we know where all of our people in New York and Washington are—whether they are in the office or not—and we have reached out to talk with each of them.
>
> For our clients, we have offered office space, recommended ways for them to participate in the recovery of New York, helped with their own internal communications, helped them put their own crisis plans into place, counseled on relief efforts, and worked closely with clients in those industries most closely affected by this tragedy such as financial services, airline, security, transportation, and travel.
>
> For these two cities, Burson-Marsteller people have walked neighborhoods to collect food for hospital and rescue workers, collected tee-shirts and socks, donated blood, worked switchboards, and organized fund-raising to buy water for police and firefighters. In addition, we have taken the lead in reaching out to hospitals and city organizations to offer help of any kind. Moreover, one of our teams has been at the center of putting together a coalition of New York City–wide organizations that would serve as a one-source channel for marshalling the kind of support that will be needed for rebuilding.
>
> In times like these, "making things happen" makes all the difference. It doesn't change what has happened but it does create purpose when everything around almost seems to stand still.

On September 21, a good friend of mine, a New York City police officer, took me to Ground Zero, the center of the tragedy. I'm not sure I was
permitted to be there but we had talked and he said he would take me with
him when he went to work early that morning, moving debris and searching for victims. When I came back to the office, I met with our human
resource team. I couldn't hold back the tears and I cried. I had served as a
combat helicopter pilot but had never seen destruction that vast or devastating to so many in one place. In my e-mail to the worldwide team that
afternoon, I wrote:

> Hours before dawn this morning in a light rain, I was escorted
> through a series of police barricades below Canal Street in
> Manhattan to "Ground Zero."
>
> The physical destruction is beyond belief.
>
> Rounding the corner, walking through the mud, the first eyeful hits
> you and you realize that no picture and no film footage could
> really share the depth of this terrible act. You can't get your bear-
> ings . . . and you don't even know which building is what any
> longer. The twisted steel, concrete, and glass that were once build-
> ings as high as 108 floors are now no more than ten stories high
> but go eight stories below the surface. The smoke still rises, the
> rubble burns beneath the ground, and it is so hot where the PATH
> trains used to run that not even rats can live. One of the buildings
> that still stands—but with shattered walls and thousands of broken
> windowpanes—has a shard of steel sticking out the side. That 30-
> foot piece of steel was once a beam in one of the Twin Towers a
> block away.
>
> But when you look, what you also see is something special.
>
> What you see is the sheer power of muscle and spirit.
>
> The search for survivors, the removal of debris, the determination
> on faces, the command posts, the support services, the literally tons
> of supplies donated from around the country and around the
> world—these are not the things of destruction but of caring and

willpower. My friend, the police officer who escorted me down this morning, told me of how he and others had worked day after day in teams handing debris from one to another, literally piece by piece to clear the wreckage in the search for survivors.

"Ground Zero" literally has become a city within a city, everything you need to function and everyone focused on a task . . . everyone focused on recovery and then healing. This is an army in action. It's what I know from my own experience 30 years ago.

And in those faces, that determination is very personal.

That's what it will take. For each of us. Personal commitment and determination.

If there ever was a time when communication is vital it is during a crisis. The unknown is fearful. Expectation is agonizing. An absence of credible information encourages the mind to wander and the worry becomes mind-numbing. Every rumor, every nugget of information—real or imagined—takes on a credibility that none deserve. And every possible scenario fights for attention, sometimes the most dramatic winning the day and capturing attention.

Yet it is not enough just to provide information. Communication during those times is much more. It must speak to both the facts and the heart. It means being calm, but not without concern and emotion. More than anything, it is a means of helping people by putting the situation into perspective so that they can hear, internalize, and then act on the information they receive.

Speaking with emotion will capture attention and give others a very personal perspective to consider. That kind of communication means words that are genuine, free-flowing, and sometimes in short sentences, much like listening to someone speak.

The challenge is always not being sure that you got through to those who are reading or listening. Simply put, you have to trust your gut . . . speak from your gut. And believe that your honest feelings will make a difference.

My writings were not the only ones. I was joined by other senior members of our team. They spoke in ways that created hope and promise. All of our leaders spoke with deep conviction to their teams and the company at large. And managers everywhere talked openly about what they felt.

Within days, we began to hear back and learned whether our combined communications were as helpful as we meant them to be.

From our Latin America region, one person wrote us: "When we are 'in the trenches,' it is inspirational to hear your observations and feelings from your heart. . . . Your efforts are felt all over our region."

From Asia, another sent an e-mail to us: "Your priorities are clear. . . . We feel cared for, valued, taken care of, and safe. Your regard for our people, our clients, respect for their/our emotions, helping each of us overcome and reach out during this time is extraordinary."

From Miami, one wrote: "What we at B-M have proven in the most ordinary circumstances—that we are a single company and a single team—seems even more evident and visible in this, the most extraordinary of times."

And from another part of the world, we heard: "Speaking personally, I think what you said today and how you said it was very comforting, supportive, and meaningful."

When the immediacy of September 11 passed, we put together a binder for the firm. In it we placed all the e-mails—from us and to us—that were written during that period. We called the collection *The Power of the Human Spirit*. It served to honor the contributions made by so many and the character that people showed.

With time, people forget the specifics. But what they remember is the personal communication—the individual and genuine emotion that resonates with them. If communication has an ultimate goal, it is to make people strong and valued. They, in turn, will foster a reputation—personal and organizational—in which value, character, individual effort, and caring are at the top of the chart.

NOTE

1. Ivo Bozon, "McKinsey conversations with global leaders: Jeroen van der Veer of Shell," *McKinsey Quarterly*, www.mckinseyquarterly.com, July 2009.

chapter 6

Seek to Understand

I am an inveterate seeker of answers. I need to understand and cannot rest with just accepting what I am told. My view is that, if I don't really grasp what a particular financial product is designed to do, I am not comfortable. Relentless is a pretty good word to describe the way I approach the communication I have with my clients.
                    —Jettie Edwards, independent consultant and mutual fund board member

NONE OF US WILL ever have all the answers when we face new challenges. Most of the time, we look to have a clear idea of the critical issues, a laser-like focus on the objective, and a sense of the path we want to take.

Long before I became a helicopter pilot, I first read the writings of Antoine de Saint-Exupéry, the historic French writer and aviator who started his career in 1926 flying the mail from France to what was then French West Africa and later on to South America. He would go on to fly in World War II for the French partisans, his plane disappearing during a reconnaissance flight in mid-1944, never to be found again.

Although he would become more famous for *The Little Prince*, I loved his trilogy, *Airman's Odyssey*. At the beginning of *Wind, Sand and Stars*, he tells a story of the apprehension he felt when getting ready for his solo flight to Dakar.

> Now it was my turn to take on at dawn the responsibility of a cargo of passengers and the African mails. But at the same time I felt very meek. I felt myself ill-prepared for this responsibility. Spain was poor in emergency fields; we had no radio; and I was troubled lest when I got into difficulty I should not know where to hunt a landing-place. I fled to spend this night vigil with my friend Guillaumet. I should have to be initiated by Guillaumet.
>
> When I walked in he looked up and smiled.
>
> "I know all about it," he said. "How do you feel?"
>
> Guillaumet exuded confidence the way a lamp gives off light. He was himself later on to break the record for postal crossings in the Andes and the South Atlantic. On this night, sitting in his shirtsleeves, his arms folded in the lamplight, smiling the most heartening of smiles, he said to me simply:
>
> "You'll be bothered from time to time by storms, fog, snow. When you are, think of those who went through it before you, and say to yourself: 'What they could do, I can do.'" [1]

For me—beyond identifying with another pilot's fears and then hearing the wisdom shared by the more experienced pilot—this story is about admitting our own vulnerability. Saint-Exupéry says he "felt very meek." Most of us do at times. And we need the input of others. Moreover, we need the help of a Guillaumet . . . one or many more.

When I was promoted to worldwide chief executive, it was a humbling moment. A little frightening too. I had some ideas but not nearly enough. When it came time to turn my attention to our European operations, I pulled together the senior team so that we could talk about what lay ahead and our goals and strategies for the coming year.

At the outset of our meeting, I retold this same story from Saint-Exupéry. It was my way of acknowledging my own vulnerability and my way to ask for input, advice, and, most important, a dialog. It was a chance for me to encourage communication to help me hear from others and to learn.

The meeting, though, was simply a start. Nothing extraordinary happened that evening. But it began a search for a deeper understanding and a way of communicating that lasted for years. In it, we all learned from each other. And a reputation for wanting help and seeking answers from others started to take shape.

Listen First . . . Talk Second

In all of communication—in all of engagement —the most important lesson for achieving results and building reputation in the process is the simple idea that you must have a conversation—a dialog—with those you work with and for. You don't dominate and neither do they. If all you do is remember one concept surrounding the importance of communication to success, remember this: *Listen first . . . talk second.*

Whether you are an established manager or an entrepreneur, one of the greatest qualities you can develop is to let others have their say.

But why is listening and letting others talk so important?

There are two perspectives. First, what do you get from listening? And second, what do the people with whom you talk learn because you listen?

Listening to people:

I Gives you access to new ideas.

I Gives you access to different perspectives.

I Moves you beyond your own vulnerability as you see that others care as much as you.

I Makes you feel you have partners in addressing problems.

I Underscores the fact that you respect and value the opinions of others.

For others, your listening:

I Makes them feel that their ideas are worthy.

I Says to them that you want their advice.

I Reinforces the importance of others to the success of the enterprise.

▌ Encourages them to think through what they have to say.

▌ Starts a process in which others know they will be asked for their views and, as a result, they plan for it, giving the process more thought than they might have otherwise.

▌ Puts pressure on them to come forward with their own thinking.

▌ Solidifies their role on a team, making them responsible.

▌ Ensures that they cannot be bystanders to what needs to be done.

▌ Isolates them if they do not contribute.

▌ Bonds them to the final decision.

When you look at this list, what strikes you? Clearly, listening can have as meaningful an impact on others as it does for you. That is good for the enterprise and enhances your reputation. If others feel better after being with you, that says a lot about you and your approach to those with whom you work.

What is required to truly listen? It takes two things. First, pay attention . . . seriously, really pay attention. If you don't it is worse than not listening at all.

Second, and equally important, take notes. A remarkable thing happens when you take notes. On the one hand, you actually pay closer attention; on the other, the individual talking is likely to speak more clearly and logically than he or she might do otherwise. Plus, it is a very visible sign that you care about what that person has to say.

Don't Be a "Know-It-All"

No one likes people who think they have all the answers. If being a partner means sharing ideas and joining together in working to reach a common objective, a "know-it-all" will have to go it alone. Such people remain aloof figures who dominate and intimidate, even if they do it subtly. Those around them feel alienated, as if their contribution doesn't matter. No one wants to work under, work with, or hire a know-it-all. Staff feels squashed. Coworkers feel undervalued. And clients are never sure whether the person is truly working with their interests in mind.

Your reputation as a professional depends in great measure upon your ability to partner with others. If you come across as thinking you have all the answers, you will earn a reputation for not being a team player, and in today's work environment that is the kiss of death to your career.

The surest way to demonstrate to others that you value their partnership is to include them in discussions, have them probe possible solutions, and look for answers with you. When you take the time to ask questions because you genuinely want the input, give those with whom you work the time to share their ideas in full. This simple act of openness and patience demonstrates respect for their views and serves as a strong statement of your confidence in their ability to think through potential initiatives and action steps.

Give People Face Time

In today's busy world, time often necessitates that getting input and ideas from others takes place through e-mail or on conference calls. This works well under some circumstances, but for the most significant issues it won't suffice.

Claude Ritman, executive director of Coler-Goldwater Hospital in New York City, can't emphasize this enough.

> I meet with family members, communicate with front-line staff, and never rely solely on written reports. There is nothing like meeting face-to-face... that is the most immediate and the most effective way of getting feedback.

The lesson is that you should not let important issues rest without an in-person discussion. E-mail—just like memos of yesteryear—can be seen as very impersonal and often come across as *fait accompli*. There is no better way to address an important issue and demonstrate a human approach to your business role than getting together in one room to discuss important decisions, strategies, and initiatives.

Ask Lots of Questions

If you want to encourage a thoughtful and productive dialog and engage with people in a way that will produce the best thinking—therefore, the best ideas—the depth of the questions you ask of your team to stimulate discussion will make a big difference.

Alberto Ibarguen, president and chief executive of the Knight Foundation, emphasizes that you have to ask questions if you are to develop an accurate and in-depth perspective on a situation. Those insights, coupled with an openness to new ideas, expand the range of possibilities . . . and the sky's the limit for what you can accomplish.

> That means you ask questions to find out more, you challenge the status quo, and you work hard to learn what might be, not what is or what was.

As we all know, there is nothing quite as powerful as a series of well-thought-through questions. And that requires preparation. A lot of it.

Journalists and attorneys come first to mind as among the most skilled at thinking through situations and pulling together probing questions. From both, we can take some guidance. History and the time-honored traditions of the "fourth estate" give reporters a particular vantage point for ensuring that facts are uncovered and people are accountable for their actions. And, with a disciplined approach relying on deliberate and exhaustive research of facts, figures, and precedent, attorneys become very adept at uncovering insights that might otherwise be missed.

What we learn from both reporters and attorneys is the following:

I Think through various scenarios beforehand.

I Perform your research.

I Be organized in the kinds of questions you ask.

I Probe and probe some more. Dig deep.

I Don't take "it can't be" as an answer.

I Look for other ideas, even when the first responses sound "good enough."

I Examine the issue from different angles.

I Ask the "what if's."

I Open the discussion so everyone can comment and ask their own questions.

❙ Ask . . . and ask again.

Jettie Edwards says that intellectual curiosity, relentless communication, and personal reputation are the cornerstones of her professional relationships and her career:

> If I go in to see a portfolio manager who is just about ready to package a fixed income product, for example, I need to understand why it was packaged that way and what about it is going to work for the investor.
>
> My process is pretty fixed. I always ask tons of questions. Listen. Ask more questions. Absorb what I have been told and then prepare my recommendation or assessment.
>
> Very specifically, when I go to speak with a manager, these are my action steps. I ask for all the written materials with the underlying research. Next, I interview the manager, probing as deeply as I can until I think there is no stone left unturned. Not stopping there, I also interview everyone I can who touched the creation of that particular product. I take on a tough, "show me" attitude, not because I want to be nasty but because it is my responsibility to understand both "why" and "how." Without those insights—built on engaging directly with those who matter—I don't believe I can properly fulfill my role and provide the kind of recommendations that will be valued and, in fact, prove themselves over time.

When you ask questions, as Edwards points out next, you need to offer a secure sense that candor and openness will be protected. In other words, when asking probing questions, you can ensure that the answers will be more truthful if there is an environment of security and trust.

> Those interviews are never as a group but rather only as one-on-ones . . . and they are never "for attribution." I need candor and the confidence that what I hear is only for my research and evaluation purposes. If anyone were to think that what they said would be misused, my ability to be successful is diminished.

When my research and discussions are complete, I come back with my analysis. Since I am independent, there are times when I have to tell the manager that "he has an ugly baby," meaning that the product won't work. Not a fun message but, then again, it is my job. My reputation—and credibility—rests on trust and values. Without them, I am lost.

Candor is a two-way street. Coworkers and clients need it in order to give you all the information you need to do your job effectively. In turn, you need to speak candidly to keep things honest and on track with reality. Candor implies that respect and trust are present. These are things a good reputation can nurture, and which in turn create a great basis for your reputation.

Keep It Practical: Ask for Examples

Probing and asking questions are key. But so is asking for examples. You have to push it one step further so that people are pressed to make it practical. It is those examples that make it real.

Harvey Rosenthal, retired president and board member of CVS, had this to say:

I'm not a very abstract thinker. So my management style was always to ask, "Can you give me an example of what you mean?" Those examples were important to me. They forced each observation, idea, or recommendation to be practical because you had to think through how it would actually work or what actually happened. You had to work through the details. It couldn't be just abstract.

In my view, it was important to keep it practical, not theoretical. So, I asked a lot of questions. My goal was to better understand what was being presented and, in the process, to make sure that those presenting really understood the details themselves. Those examples were powerful teaching tools about what would work and what wouldn't.

This kind of practical approach—with probing questions—became part of my reputation. In the end, I think we were better prepared as a company and the management team was better prepared. When forced to give examples, it forced a clearer understanding. And that served us all well.

Even though I asked a lot of questions, I really was quiet and low-key. It was the way I worked and it seemed to fit what was expected of a small, modest company with a strong tradition of getting close to the customer.

Asking for examples is a great way to mine the past for lessons and to explore new avenues for your particular task. It not only reveals methods you can apply, but also helps the person describing the situation to think things through more fully. As Rosenthal points out, it keeps things practical. In business, having a reputation for being practical is an asset.

Effective communication comes from understanding. By seeking to understand where people are coming from and by getting to the root of their intentions and ideas, you form a strong basis for all communication. And you will earn a reputation as someone who respects the people you work with.

If you take the time and energy to understand people, they will believe in you... in great measure because you show that you believe in them. You probe. You ask. You develop an appreciation for their thinking and their energy. They can feel it. They can see it. And, because of the attention you paid to them and their ideas, they know you mean it. In exchange for your loyalty to them, they will be loyal to you.

Once you have gathered people's thoughts, opinions, ideas, suggestions, special needs, and inspirations it is up to you to consider what they have said and to reach a point of decision on how to act on it. On the most basic level, when you understand where they are coming from, communicating your own ideas and decisions becomes easier. You know how to approach people individually and they, in turn, are better able to listen and truly hear what you have to say. This is why understanding people forms the basis for everything else in this book's section on communication.

In the next two chapters, you will not only learn methods for communicating effectively. You will also learn the fine art of engaging people in your endeavor. This team approach involves others and helps spread the word that you are someone to partner with to accomplish a common goal.

NOTE

1. Antoine de Saint-Exupéry, *Airman's Odyssey* (New York: Reynal & Hitchcock, 1932), p. 6.

chapter 7

Effective Communication

I have long believed that appropriate behavior is at the core of "a good name" or a strong reputation. Appropriate behavior, effectively communicated, will result in favorable public acceptance—another way of saying that it will create and sustain a favorable reputation.
—Harold Burson, founder of Burson-Marsteller

HAVE YOU EVER watched yourself on video?

It is an eye-opening experience. I've been taped and been on broadcast talk shows many times. The first time is always quite a shock, especially when you take a critical look at yourself.

Leading a meeting or talking with your colleagues is no different. All eyes are on you. You are center stage. Every movement, every smile, every frown, and every hand gesture is under scrutiny.

I remember once working with a client who was under attack by the media for the side effects of a prescription drug. The client was a physician and we were preparing him for a broadcast appearance on the famed and feared *60 Minutes*. He was to be interviewed in order to explain the exhaustive testing of the drug, the patient feedback, and the FDA approvals. We knew that his appearance on the show would merely be the starting point for discussion about his credibility, his credentials, and his reputation . . . in the traditional media, on the Internet, and among the social networking media. In turn, we knew that his being on the show was critical to ensuring a balanced understanding of drug testing, risk, side effects, drug disclosure, and patient experience.

In the best tradition of media coaching, we re-created a traditional *60 Minutes* stage set, with its unique camera angles and interviewer positioning. The lights were hot, the set was crowded with people, and it couldn't have been more uncomfortable for our client. Add to the physical discomfort the fact that the questions were brutal, direct, and fast and furious. We were very harsh on him. Don't squirm in the chair. Don't cover your mouth. Speak clearly. Look directly at the camera and the interviewer. Think before you talk. Be pleasant. Feel comfortable. Answer with authority. And draw on the facts.

Did he do well in the training and rehearsal? Yes. In three hours, he had made real progress. He looked at himself in the video replays. He cringed, yet it was clear that he had improved considerably.

But he hated every minute of it. In fact, when I walked him off the set that afternoon, he said to me, "This was the most intimidating moment in my life. It was disrespectful to me. It was a waste of time. And I will never speak to you again. You're fired."

Regardless of his anger with me and his fondest wish not to be interviewed the next morning, the interview was set and he had no choice but to appear. He knew that by skipping the interview, the camera would focus in on an empty chair on the set and the interviewer would roast him, his company, and his reputation like never before. Running never works. And an appearance "in absentia" never works.

Needless to say, he went to the interview the next morning at 9:30. It lasted about an hour. By the time the segment aired, his time on camera would be cut to less than ten minutes. But he did it.

At 11:15, I received a call on my cell. It was the very same physician. He had two words to say: "Thank you." He went on to say that the preparation was horrible but the learnings were so important. It had given him a preview of how he would appear, and he had come to realize that how he came across would be the critical factor that gave credibility to his words. During the evening between the coaching session and the actual interview, he had been introspective. He thought through the impression he would give and how the images and the words needed to be one and the same.

This physician's lesson—made all the more dramatic because *60 Minutes,* often called America's #1 news program, has more than 10 million viewers—applies to every individual who wants to ensure that he or she builds a sense of common understanding. The words, the voice, the body language, all must come together.

So too with you, whenever you communicate. Your reputation depends on it and, in turn, so does your success.

The Call for Serious and Transparent Communications

Today's digital communication and media environment—and the expanded access to information they have spawned—have changed the way that people communicate. Information travels at lightning speed. Blogs, social networking, Facebook, Twitter, instant messaging, and other channels for online commentary have all created a world where anyone can be a self-professed expert, say virtually anything, share their thinking, and comment on issues ranging from global politics to corporate ethics to small-town high school football games. Tapping on a keyboard, even in the dark of night, everyone has a voice today and a soapbox from which to speak.

Communication has become serious business and the pressures on you to participate and respond are intense. As we see virtually every day, not communicating our views on key issues or in reply to important questions is tantamount to No Comment. That, as we know, is never helpful.

In a *McKinsey Quarterly* interview, Jeroen van der Veer, retired CEO of Royal Dutch Shell, strongly urged managers to take communication seriously because of the expectations that others—both employees and outside stakeholders—had about performance and results:

> Not only internal communication—people feel uncertain, so they like to understand how the bosses think about it—but external: with politicians, ministers. And nearly every discussion you start in the first two minutes with not necessarily the subject you have to discuss, but [instead with]: "What do you think? How long will it

last?" And people, they expect an answer. You better think about that. So you have to think a lot about communication. Externally and internally, what are your key messages? [1]

There is no question that we are in a demanding era, especially for communication. There is no substitute for informed conversation and open dialog against a backdrop of disclosure and speed. The expectation of those who work with us is for us to be honest, transparent, and genuinely compassionate of others. When openness is missing, it creates the kind of doubt and skepticism that will undermine our efforts to be successful.

With such easy access by everyone to a wide range of traditional, online, social networking, and other communication methods and tools, the common assumption is that if we don't use them to their fullest extent, we are either afraid of dialog or trying purposely to avoid potentially sensitive or troublesome issues. The result is an immediate and full-on blow to our reputation that could damage our credibility and our ability to work with people effectively.

There is no substitute for communication that is responsible, integrity-based, honest, candid, and transparent—and that, as a result, reflects the reputation you want to create. Likewise, to be effective in this era of instant information and to successfully communicate the attributes that differentiate our reputation, we must take full advantage of technology and the digital world so that our messages and points of view and the reasoning behind our management decisions reach those who matter and, ultimately, will pass judgment on our words and actions.

Communication and Retention

People often assume that the way they see others is an accurate portrayal. In many cases they may be right, but looks can be deceiving. The simple reason for this is that we all bring our own particular perspective and preconceived ideas to the interpretation of what we see. In other words, we bring our personal bag and baggage to how we perceive things.

We need to remember that the mind doesn't always work in rational or logical ways. This makes it even more important for us to try to grasp how others see us, what they think of us, what they remember about us, how they paint a picture of us, and, as a result, what they believe about us.

Experts caution that we see things in snapshots, often little bits at a time. We remember glimpses of an image or an idea, but rarely the full picture. We hear a little of what was said, not the entire comment. Often, we lose the context or disregard what else is going on. Sometimes, we simply might not see the entire picture or we choose to ignore some of what we have learned or heard. In other situations, our reaction might be emotional rather than rational. We may completely misunderstand something because we made judgments without the facts.

Most people, experts say, only retain ten percent of what they hear when someone else is speaking. Subjective listening is part of it. The other part is that we can only retain so much at any given time. Whether we like it or not, this is human behavior and we have to understand it and work with it.

Speaking to Be Heard

Speechwriters know the art of communication well. It's one of the reasons they are fond of short sentences. They take complex topics and break them into small, easily understandable parts . . . almost like cutting a large piece of steak into small bites so that it can be chewed and digested more easily.

Those same speechwriters use memorable words and well-crafted phrases that have an impact on the listener by conjuring images or feelings that touch an emotional chord.

Presidential speechwriters are some of the very best. They know how to turn a phrase, create a picture, and leave a lasting impression. They, in fact, know well how to grab the listener's attention by asking a provocative question, sharing a series of thoughts, and expressing emotion. They pay great attention to each word because they know that whatever the president says will be scrutinized, leave a lasting impression, and serve to build a reputation.

Even if you aren't the president of the United States or the president of your organization, you need to apply the same skills to how you phrase whatever it is that you want to say and write. Both require considerable thought and clarity. Think about your words. What do they mean? Equally important, how will they be interpreted? One of the great challenges of the English language is that so many words have more than one meaning, some actual and direct and others by implication, suggestion, or context. Your choice of words is so important.

So how do you apply those skills as you build your own reputation? Here are some ideas:

❙ *Paint images when you talk and outline plans.* People respond to imagery. They can see pictures. They can see themselves in those pictures. If you are starting a business, help others picture what the business will be like when it grows, expands, and they have an increasingly important role. Help them imagine what it will mean to them. If you are an entrepreneur and you are meeting with those who can provide financial support, help them see what the future will be like when you are successful and help them think about what that will mean.

❙ *Name those who are essential to your success.* Involve those with whom you work on a personal basis. Talk about the special skills and dedication that they bring to the enterprise and what their work means to success. Point them out by name so that you capture their excitement and their loyalty. Give credit to them. It will bring credit to you. As I've said before, you get more than you give when you share credit and loyalty.

❙ *Always refer to "the team."* Teams create success more often than do individuals alone. Talk about the team's contributions to the goal and the team's dedication to success. Involve others, whether they are your staff, your clients, your vendors, or even your bosses.

❙ *Invoke those who have been successful before you.* Use examples of people who have tried and succeeded before you. Talk about what they have done that has made them stand out.

❙ *Use emotionally laden words like "courage," "determination," "strength," "loyalty," and "new frontiers."* Capture excitement by making the people you work with see themselves as pioneers with that same spirit. Help them view what they are doing as something special . . . but difficult. In many ways, the harder the challenge, the harder people will work and fight for what they think they can accomplish.

❙ *Speak from personal experience.* If the military was part of your background, invoke images from those experiences. If sailing is your passion, use imagery from the challenges of sailors, high winds, and high seas. If literature is what gives you inspiration, talk about what you have learned from historians, authors, and poets. If nature is key to the way you live your life, create images that others can see and that give them a unique perspective.

ı *And most of all, speak from the heart.* Don't be trite. Speak from what you know and what you most care about. Talk about personal values, family, honor, and sharing success and do it with conviction and passion. And don't be afraid to show emotion.

These are some of the techniques of the best speechwriters. Use them well. And use them wisely to engage people in your enterprise.

Straight Talk . . . No Spin

If perception and reality are to align, then there is no substitute for straight talk.

John S. Knight—best known as Jack Knight—was one of the toughest newspaper owners in the United States but he also was one of the most admired. He had this to say about the reputation he worked for:

> I want to have a reputation of being fair and honorable and doing the right thing. Printing good newspapers. Being objective and opinionated.[2]

To put muscle around his convictions on the importance of reputation, Jack went on to relay what happened when, after taking Knight-Ridder public, he sat down to meet with Wall Street security analysts for the first time.

> I made the first talk at the security analysts, and the last talk I ever made. I was never invited again. My opening line was, "Ladies and Gentlemen, I do not intend to become your prisoner." A gal about 26 was sitting next to me and said "That a boy, baby, that's great." I told them why. I said, as long as I had anything to do with it, we were going to run the papers, we were going to spend money sometimes that they wouldn't understand why we were spending it, for future gains, and we did not intend to be regulated, or

directed by them in any respect. That's pretty challenging isn't it? It was the right thing to say, too.[3]

Jack Knight's style was to be direct. As for his reputation, he wanted to be known as "fair and honorable and doing the right thing. . . . Being objective and opinionated."

That he surely was.

Simply put, Jack Knight tackled them head-on. He had the courage not to shy away from reality. This was his commitment to telling it like it is. His straightforward approach would pay off in many ways, not the least among them respect and reputation.

Straight talk means no "spin." There's no room for trying to twist the facts, avoid the issue, shade the truth, or walk away from reality. To cut to the chase: the concept of spin is disrespectful. It flies in the face of trust and is devoid of integrity.

Whether used as a noun or a verb, the word *spin* implies that the people with whom you want to communicate aren't capable of real understanding. Spin means that, somehow, you believe they are incapable of distinguishing fact from fiction and they are easily manipulated into believing what you say and, ultimately, agreeing. In short, it means you think they are not very bright.

When it comes to relating to anyone in business—whether clients or coworkers—straight talk must rule the day. There is no place for spin, or anything like it.

Think about it this way: If straight talk is what CEOs need to do when speaking with those who make investment decisions or make *buy, sell,* or *hold* recommendations about their stock—and, in turn, influence the company's financial future—then you should do no less when it comes to working with the people who make the products or sell the services that serve as the foundation of your company's success.

If your choice is to try to spin it, remember the warning of the Italian proverb that, when literally translated, goes like this: *Deceit has short legs.* Or in the more colloquial version: *You can't run from the truth.*

As we all know, it's never if the truth will be known . . . but rather just *when.*

Words and Actions in Lockstep

The words you use and your behavior must always be in sync. They must reflect both the values you hold dear and the principles on which you build your reputation. In everything you do and say, your goal should be that perception and reality are one and the same, building a reputation that will serve you well throughout your career.

When deciding what you will do, what you will say, and how you will speak, you should view those actions through a lens that can anticipate and interpret how others are likely to react. Simply put, everyone is watching you closely. And they will make judgments. Clearly, if you want to ensure your success, you should never do or say anything that contradicts the particular qualities and values that underscore the reputation you so desire and need.

If everyone is watching what you do and say, you cannot afford a misstep. You cannot afford a blow to your reputation—perceived or otherwise. Every step of the way, you must be seen to be genuine and your actions in keeping with your reputation.

Body Language

How others see you with their eyes is almost as important a factor in how they perceive you as what they hear from you with their ears. Your body language speaks loudly about your reputation—about whether you are genuine, about the depth of your convictions, and about whether you are being open and forthright. Together with what you say, how you behave when you say it does matter. In fact, it matters a great deal.

Communication takes many forms: Your words, which others hear. Your movements, which others see . . . even the smallest ones, such as a turn of your head, the movement of your hand, or the blink of your eye. These things are noticed and send a message.

Like my client, the physician, who went through training and had the benefit of watching himself on camera, you can do the same. And you don't need a television studio to rehearse and see yourself. A digital camera that takes short movies will do well. With prices at less than $100, they are within everyone's reach.

So think about how you look to others when they are watching you. Think about your body language. Think about the impact the following kinds of movements have and the image they communicate:

▎*The Smirk.* You twist your mouth. That little movement with your lips and everyone knows you are disdainful of what someone else has said. Did you really mean it that way? Or were you just not paying attention and your reaction got the better of you? Think about those involuntary movements and work to control them. They do matter.

▎*The Slouch.* Were you sitting straight up and listening intently? Or were you slouching in the chair, almost without a care in the world or, even worse, with little care or interest in what the other person was saying? As we teach our children, sit up straight, sit in the front row, and pay attention.

▎*The Squirm.* How about squirming? Did you sit still or did you bounce around, looking left and right, almost as if you were avoiding the discussion or trying to sneak away? Remember, you are there for a reason. Others take their guidance from you . . . so concentrate. Pay attention and focus.

▎*The Swipe.* You were asked a tough question. You took some time to answer it . . . and then you couldn't help yourself. Your hand wiped across your mouth. A classic movement that tells everyone you had to "wipe off" what you just said. Likely, your answer wasn't genuine. The impression is that you just lied or, at the very least, shaded the truth. Watch what you say. Be straightforward and candid. If you are, the rest of your body won't be tempted to "wipe it off."

▎*The Eyeballs.* More than any other part of our body, the eyes have it. They speak loudly. They light up when you are enthusiastic. They communicate caring and strength when you look directly into another's eyes. They wander when your mind wanders. And they close when you are bored or simply don't care. Pay attention. Look closely at others with whom you work and those you want to work with you and follow your direction. Don't let those eyes stray. Most of all, remember that they tell the truth. When you look straight ahead, directly at those who are important, your eyes speak of a direct, attentive, and caring approach. When your eyes drop down to the side after you have spoken, they often tell others that you are running away from what you just said. In other words, you have fudged the truth. Remember the English proverb: "The eyes are the window to the soul."

I *The Hands.* Oh, the hands. From the firm handshake that communicates character and strength of personality to gestures that emphasize points you want to make, your hands are emotive. They add conviction and enthusiasm. They emphasize. Use them wisely and use them well, because they are powerful adjectives adding color and meaning to the words you use.

When you think about effective communication—all geared toward the kind of reputation that will help you accomplish what you want—think about how others see you. What does your body language tell them? And is it what you want them to hear . . . or see?

Communicate by Example

Harold Burson is very clear about the relationship among behavior, communication, and reputation.

In his essay titled *Civil Disobedience* (1849), Henry David Thoreau said it right: "It is truly enough said that a corporation has no conscience; but a corporation of conscientious men is a corporation with a conscience."

For the corporation, the big question is: "What constitutes appropriate behavior?" I have long believed the chief executive officer sets the tone for the company. If his or her custom is to arrive at the office at 7:00 in the morning, direct reports will arrive at 6:45. If he or she is profligate in his business entertainment, subordinates will follow the example. If he or she strongly supports a policy of diversity in employee hiring and promotions, that policy is likely to prevail at all levels of the business. If he or she regularly engages with customers, that action will influence the behavior of those in marketing, sales, and service.

The "little things" also count. Does the CEO have lunch in the company cafeteria or only in an executive dining room? Does he or she occasionally "walk the floors" at corporate headquarters and visit outlying plants and other facilities? Does the CEO use a special elevator or ride with the "herd"?

All of these go into the amalgam that makes for that "good name."

On a personal basis and as a guiding principle for the firm I founded, I always believed that how a company treats its employees—and their families by extension—is the single most important factor that an "outsider" uses to reach judgment about a company.

I, for one, would never ask anything of others that I wouldn't do myself. I always managed against a foundation of values that I believed would endure. And I believed in sharing the opportunities with the others in the team. When I eventually sold the company, there were 110 other employees who had an ownership stake in the firm.

And even today, I still always answer my own phone and my office door is always open.

It's all about making people know they are part of the team. It's about motivating, even inspiring employees at all levels to know that the primary objective for the company is its good name.

While Harold Burson talks about the example set by a CEO, that very same behavior is what every person at every level should do to set an example. He provides four important lessons for everyone who understands the importance of reputation:

1. Behavior is what others see. It is what drives support, loyalty, and a common bond. It is what creates a "good name."

2. That bond and that "good name" build a reputation. If done well over time, that reputation endures.

3. Humility is at the core of the best of reputations . . . never ask another to do what you wouldn't do yourself.

4. Success is a team effort. When the team is motivated and inspired, they focus as one on the "good name" . . . on reputation. And success follows.

The Power of Information to Educate and Increase Awareness

Good reputations are not built in a vacuum. Rather, good reputations are built over time and are based on what people hear and experience and how they evaluate why things are done in a certain way. Information—communicated in an open and engaging manner—is critical to that process.

Information creates the basis on which people have the opportunity to understand what you do and why you do it. That information educates others, helps them understand what is being done and why, and increases awareness so understanding comes more easily. Therefore your goal should be to educate, inform, build understanding, and increase awareness at every opportunity.

Rose Mann, assistant dean of advancement for the Rosenstiel School of Marine and Atmospheric Science, sees a very close link between effective organizational communication and the success of her work. A strong reputation—made visible by an effective communication program that informs, educates, and increases awareness of both the organization and the individual—creates success.

> One member of my staff is a communication professional. If we don't do what we say we are going to do and keep the donors informed, those who give will stop and we will have failed. So our credibility—personal and professional—is vital. Beyond that, we have to communicate about the exciting research findings and the new developments going on at the school. This kind of communication builds the framework within which we can be successful. Donors will know more about Rosenstiel. They will have a feeling for what is going on. And they can start imagining what kind of role they can play if the school is seen as exciting and dynamic, making major contributions to marine life.

Strong and effective communication delivers information in ways that are interesting and in ways that reach out to others. As a result, that kind of communication is at the core of a strong reputation and a successful career.

When most people think of communication, their first thoughts often gravitate to the many techniques used by businesses to communicate with a wide range of stakeholders. The value there seems to be clearer and more easily grasped. Perhaps it is because we often hear about communication and public relations departments and the many ways they engage employees, shareholders and investors, key decision makers, politicians, strategic partners, members of their local communities, and, of course, customers or clients. Some of the techniques—both traditional and digital—we hear about are:

- Social media campaigns

- Newsletters

- E-mail blasts (e-blasts)

- Press releases

- Marketing initiatives

- Briefings

- Press conferences

- Online and traditional media campaigns

- Lobbying efforts

- Government relations

- Outreach to online social networking media, such as Facebook, Twitter, LinkedIn, blogs, and websites

- Public speeches

- Advertising and paid media

- Publicity campaigns

Without information, there can be no basis on which people can make a judgment. Or, in the absence of an understanding, people don't understand and will simply make up answers to why you do what you do. When that happens, you lose control over shaping how you are perceived and, therefore, lose control over your reputation.

These methods are critical to the success and the reputation of businesses today. And in many ways, they are essential to our individual efforts as we build our careers and enhance our individual reputations.

Preparing for Important Meetings and Discussions

When people think of practice, the image that emerges most often is from sports. When they think of rehearsals, the theater comes to mind. And when they think of preparation, important presentations with Microsoft PowerPoint documents and financial plans flash before their eyes.

In my experience, even those events that might at first appear to be the most casual of meetings and discussions deserve as much practice, rehearsal, and preparation as do major presentations. That planning leads to success. You might call it "mental rehearsal" or "mental practice" or "mental preparation."

This means planning thoroughly before the event. And it means being thoughtful, long before your thinking may be needed. Why should you take the time to do this? The crucial answer is twofold: First, regardless of the situation, your thinking must always be considered, reasoned, and reasonable; and second, the goal of any meeting is to build consensus and support.

For the latter, those with you must feel empowered if you want them to engage in a discussion and share their views. Moreover, they must feel that their input is appreciated. To make that happen—to make others feel appreciated and empowered—here are some tips to follow:

I *Frame the discussion.* Put yourself in the other person's shoes and try to think as they do. Anticipate their views, their experience, and their perceptions. Not everyone thinks like you. So, think like them. If you can anticipate and address their concerns head-on, you will be viewed as a manager who is in tune with your team members. In the process, you will gain credibility.

I *Engage with those who are important to you.* If you need someone's participation, getting them involved is the first step. Ask them to perform research or develop a strategy or recommendation on their own. Encourage them to take on a project so they will see how much you recognize their abilities and value their views.

❙ *Consider the opinions of others.* There may be very specific points you want to make to certain people. However, before you communicate, first think about the impact your messages will have on everyone. Don't overlook any particular group or point of view. To do otherwise puts you at risk of being perceived as insensitive by some, and the perceptions of those few might then galvanize the views of many.

❙ *Be credible.* Verify all your facts. Be sure that the research and the basis of your discussion can be probed, questioned, and broken apart but the facts will still stand. Explain in detail. Be open to questions. A loss of credibility on even one minor point can undermine the entire group's opinion of you —and strike a blow to your reputation.

❙ *Think through your communication options.* Ask yourself which communication techniques are best for you, what you want to say, and whom you want to reach. Perhaps an e-mail lays out some of the discussion, giving people time to think and digest the information, and even perform some research on their own. Follow that with reference data, website links or addresses, or other information sources.

❙ *Lay out your reasoning very clearly.* Take pains to fully explain your thinking. The more complete your thought process, the better others will be able to understand your position, follow your logic, and support your view or your decision.

❙ *Talk straight.* Explain situations in clear terms. Ensure that those who must participate in decisions and their implementation understand how and why the decisions are being made. They need to hear your reasoning in clear language. Shortchanging them will only shortchange your chances of success.

❙ *Acknowledge other opinions.* When you ask for the views of others, don't slough them off. Value and acknowledge their thinking and their contributions. Ask them to do more. That kind of response from you will be very well received, encouraging them to become more involved with your project and goals.

▮ *Ask for feedback.* Your openness for feedback speaks volumes about your sense of partnership, your confidence in what you think, and the value you place on the opinions of others.

▮ *Keep in mind: Today's "water cooler" is digital.* Nearly everyone is talking to everyone else online by means of mobile devices, e-mail, text, or instant messages. This includes the people you work with, whose ability to reach more people in less time has never been easier or faster. Nothing happens without giving voice to some sort of communication using the latest in digital technology.

When I think about getting ready for discussions, meetings, and conversations, I often think of General Douglas MacArthur's words: "On the fields of friendly strife are sown the seeds that on other days and other fields will bear the fruits of victory." My goal is intense preparation. Take notes. Imagine all the questions. Let no stone go unturned. Working through the issues when the pressure is the least gives you the chance to excel when the tension and the pressures are the greatest. This is the stuff of building a reputation for preparation and thought.

When you communicate effectively and genuinely, people get a clear sense of where you are coming from. Not only are they educated about your effort, but they also come to believe in you and what you are seeking to accomplish. They feel a willingness to join you in your endeavor.

The next chapter focuses on ways to build on this genuine reputation for success by creating engagement among the people you work with and for.

NOTES

1. Ivo Bozon, "McKinsey conversations with global leaders: Jeroen van der Veer of Shell," *McKinsey Quarterly,* www.mckinseyquarterly.com, July 2009.

2. Copyright 2006 Dan Neuharth. Reprinted with permission.

3. Copyright 2006 Dan Neuharth. Reprinted with permission.

chapter 8

Engaging Others

Reputation is best built on communicating a common purpose and giving people a reason to follow another's lead. Team members are on the lookout for meaning in what they do and that is often best relayed through clear communications, powerful storytelling, and a purposeful narrative for the organization. Why else would team members pledge their time, talent, and commitment to a manager, team, organization, or client?

—Leslie Gaines-Ross, author of *CEO Capital: A Guide to Building CEO Reputation and Company Success*

WHEN I RETURNED from combat in 1970, I was a captain in the Army and assigned as an instructor pilot at the primary helicopter flight school in Fort Wolters, Texas. After two weeks spent learning the techniques for how best to teach others to fly and how to gauge a flight student's progress, the other instructors and I were ready for the students. By the time we first met them on the flight line, the new class of flight students had already spent time in the classroom.

Now, it was time for the real thing. We walked across the tarmac on the airfield and went through our preflight inspection of the aircraft. The student then climbed into the right seat of the aircraft; I stepped on the skid and climbed into the left seat.

The actual cockpit flight training began. There were lessons and practice so that the student could learn how to hover, stay in one place, turn left, turn right, back up, go forward, and take off. The student had to learn to master the throttle and the collective to control the main rotor and the pitch of the blade; the pedals for the tail rotor so the aircraft didn't spin; and the cyclic for direction. The student had to practice the maneuvers over and over again so everything worked together and the helicopter could be flown safely. Of course, every training session was punctuated by the student's surprise when suddenly the instructor would roll the throttle back to simulate an engine failure. The unexpected emergency forced the student to react by rapidly lowering the collective, pushing in the right pedal, and controlling the cyclic. Repeated regularly, these auto rotations were a key part of the training to make sure the student pilot was always at the ready to bring the helicopter down safely if the engine failed.

As you might expect given the demand for helicopter pilots at the time, the military had flight-school training down to a science. While the curricula stipulated a fixed number of hours in the classroom, when it came to actual flight time, it was up to me to decide when to let each of my students make their first "solo" flight. As a result, there eventually came a time when I would have to decide if the student could make it three times around the traffic pattern, taking off and then landing each time, without an accident or incident . . . and without me sitting in the left seat, riding through on the controls.

This meant that, before I even opened the door, unbuckled my shoulder harness, and stepped out, I had to have already judged that the student could successfully complete three landings and three takeoffs. If I judged correctly, the student went on to the next stage of flight school. If I didn't judge the flight student's abilities correctly, it could be a matter of life or death.

As time went by and each one my students completed the solo flight with no incident, I began to realize that, while my assessment of the student pilot's proficiency certainly had a bearing on when I decided to unbuckle my harness, step out and off the skid, and let the student pilot take off solo, the real test was whether I trusted my own judgment about each one's ability.

My training as a pilot and my flying experience gave me the practical skills I needed. The flight school curricula provided guidance. Yet, it really all came down to judgment and confidence in myself and my decisions. That made the difference. I started to realize that, if I didn't trust myself, then I wasn't in a position to make those kinds of tough decisions that are necessary, not only as a helicopter instructor pilot in the Army but also in other roles throughout my life.

I see little difference between this flight-instructor experience and the challenge of working with people in any type of organization.

Ultimately, it comes down to whether you have confidence in yourself and, therefore, you believe in your judgment. With that belief in yourself, you believe in your team.

And they come to believe in themselves.

At some point, to engage others, you simply need to step out of the pilot seat and trust them.

Engagement Is the New Mandate

Successful businesspeople believe in proactive and straightforward communication. They know they must master the traditional and leading-edge digital communication tools, and understand the pivotal role that communication plays in engaging others and building reputation. They genuinely want to know what others think and how committed they are. Simply put, there must be a sharing of views through substantive engagement involving team members. Dialog wins the day every time.

Successful people also know that engagement demonstrates respect between themselves and their team or clients, and generates an enthusiasm for shared strategies, tactics, and goals. They believe in trying to reach a group understanding, if not consensus and agreement, on how to move forward in reaching certain goals. If that is possible, it goes a long way toward team responsibility for the outcome.

At the same time, these businesspeople are also very candid about the fact that, while communicating through engagement is preferable—if not the mandate—it is more difficult and time-consuming than making a decision quickly but with less input and little consensus. Engagement requires more energy, thought, diplomacy, and patience than simply making a decision and moving with it. It really means that you need to invest more time, energy, and attention in listening, modifying points of view and plans, and in being willing to make even further midcourse changes. Absolute clarity and logic in the identification of goals, and the reasoning behind decisions, is the order of the day.

Engaging the people you work with can be a challenge. For those who might be somewhat insecure, it can be threatening because it forces them to delve into more detail, think harder than they might have otherwise thought necessary, and review various strategies and action steps more closely. It also requires a candid look at your own logic and thought process. That, alone, can sometimes be challenging. However, the return on this investment—especially in terms of progress, results, and support— far outweighs the extra effort.

Quite frankly, if we have not mastered the art of engagement, we are not really fully living up to our responsibilities and are leaving an important requirement for a good reputation unfulfilled. We are not doing what is expected of us and our chances of being viewed favorably are limited.

In the past, communicating in a more open and inclusive manner and fully engaging the people we work with might not have been so vital . . . or, quite possibly, we just got away without doing it. However, times have changed and no one sits back and believes what is said without some measure of skepticism and doubt. People are far more discerning and less willing to blindly accept others' viewpoints. They are quick to question. They feel empowered and informed because they have instant access to an endless supply of information and opinion on the Internet.

This very same empowerment, however, is a double-edged sword for many. While the Internet makes people feel as if they have facts and figures at their disposal 24/7, there is no filter for incoming information, meaning that the information is not necessarily correct. Opinions are sometimes shared as if they were fact, not a point of view.

Therefore, the mandate for inclusion and engagement is all that much greater. Only by having substantive discussions—serious dialog—on important topics, issues, and decisions can everyone be on the same page. Or at least, everyone will be operating from the same information so the foundation for decisions will be consistent and correct. Moreover, the inclusion of all members of the team makes for a better decision and wider commitment.

Working off the same data, everyone who works together is on equal footing to share their ideas, have their voices heard, and have their input valued. They participate more actively, eagerly look for solutions, think more discerningly, and develop greater insights. The more actively they participate, the more successful we all become.

The additional time it takes to invest in substantive discussions and probing for ideas is more than offset by what we gain through shared ideas, mutual understanding, and clarity of goals.

None of this is to suggest that we disclose confidential information and discussions or go against the expert advice of legal counsel. There clearly are situations when you will not be able to talk about or disclose certain information, because doing so would violate privacy policies, disclosure requirements, or strategic-planning needs. For those kinds of situations, you should seek guidance to ensure that everyone is using the information properly and in the best interests of the organization and its customers, clients, and stakeholders.

The bottom line is that through engaging wisely we emerge with a strengthened reputation. We are trusted. We are believable. And our communication reaches out with the objective of learning, involving others, and ensuring that we have the best insights available to us. Open communication and dialog that is consistent with behavior are critical to building the kind of reputation that will generate support and get the job done.

Motivation Is the Crucial Element

A reputation for doing the best, for engaging with those who are important to us and to the organization, for communicating in an open and constructive manner, and for genuinely caring about others starts with ourselves.

We must motivate ourselves to behave that way. If we do so, our motivation extends to others. The enthusiasm and the excitement are contagious. And nothing is impossible. Steve Joenk, president and CEO of AXA Equitable Funds Management Group, LLC, said it best:

> My goal for my career and for the careers of those who work with me is to build a reputation for thinking about "how" and "why"

things need to be done, not just "what" we have to do. I believe if we understand how and why, we will be more highly valued by the organization we work for because we are thinking people. And if people feel that they are valued for what they can do, they will be willing to do so much more.

Motivating others is not only leading by example or demonstrating by your own actions what is required for success. It is also the product of helping others discover for themselves what motivates them and, if they act on that motivation, how they can be an even more active participant in their individual career growth and in the success of the organization where they work or in the success of the organization they are launching.

The most direct way of discovering what motivates others is to ask them directly. Strange as that may seem, sometimes people haven't ever been very introspective. They've never felt the need. And maybe no one ever asked them straight out.

That process needs to be started. Maybe they just assumed that their motives were "understood." They assumed others knew why they do what they do and they never felt the need or were given a reason to explain what motivates them.

For many people, it is much easier to answer the question about "what" they do than "why" they do it. The "what" is simpler and more tangible. The "why"—or the motivation—is much more difficult, complex, and often very personal. As a result, for many, the "why" rarely gets asked.

So, to get the best out of others, you need to start by just asking, "Why?" You might be the first person to do so. Like Socrates, ask questions, some direct and some indirect so that you encourage others to delve deeper and probe into the reasons why they do what they do. In the process, they will come to better understand themselves and you will develop a deeper appreciation for each of them. Both will serve you well.

Another way of better understanding how to motivate others is to create hypothetical situations that require those who work with you to analyze a situation and propose a solution. If you manage a business or department, you can conduct training sessions and hold seminars that create scenarios in which employees, once presented with a problem, are asked to develop a solution and implement it. Some of these are very hypothetical situations, such as finding your way out of being lost in the desert. Others are practical and aligned with your business. In other words, analyze a current business problem, present a solution, and develop a plan of action.

Once again, the crucial answer is not in the actual plan of action but rather in the answer to "why" a particular individual chose a particular action. Why was this plan selected over another? What was the motivation?

The Power of Clarity and Praise

Understanding the motivations of others is important. But it is simply a starting point. The next step is equally crucial: to build on those motivations so you get the very best out of each person. Your reputation and career success depend on getting the best out of others. You are only one person and, therefore, limited in what you can accomplish on your own. As a result, you need others and you need their help. Of course, you need to motivate them. So how to do just that?

I remember running the streets of New York as one of 14,000 in the New York City Marathon more than twenty years ago. That year was my second time running that marathon and the 26.2 miles of pavement always seemed endless. I was able to keep a reasonable pace from Staten Island, across the Verrazano-Narrows Bridge, and into Brooklyn. Then, my pace started to slow on the incline of the 59th Street Bridge heading up from Queens toward Manhattan. By the time I reached the Bronx, it was clear that the last seven miles were to be the biggest challenge.

Here the mind had to carry the exhausted body and propel it forward when the muscles cried out to stop. It was then that a woman, sitting by herself on a metal dinette chair on the side of the street, held up a hand-made sign that simply read: "Yes, you can."

So, from a woman I never met who didn't even run the race, I learned that lessons come from unexpected sources and that we have to be open to them at the most unusual or difficult moments in our lives and our careers. That lesson from the streets in the Bronx was not just for this race but for life and my career.

Simply put, her sign said that it was up to me. And I could do it . . . if I wished. In part because of her, I finished the New York City Marathon that year, reaching my personal best time.

Like a race, there's a start and a finish to doing your best. The starting point is clarity of communications. And at the finish line is praise for a job well done.

If we begin with the basic understanding that most everyone wants to do the best job possible, we then need to concentrate first on being clear in our instructions and laying out the challenge. As anyone will agree, if you aren't clear in your instructions, there will be little chance of success. This is true whether you are instructing your own staff or an outside firm you have hired. If you want to be clear in how you describe the challenge, you need to have thought it through better than anyone else. You have to understand the assignment very well.

As some have said: *An unsuccessful outcome is the result of bad instructions.*

Before you set others on a particular task, ask yourself these four questions:

1. Do you really understand what you are asking someone else to do?

2. Do you have a sense of the thought process that needs to be followed?

3. Have you tried to think it through yourself . . . at least a little bit?

4. Are your instructions clear? Could you follow them yourself?

Waiting at the finish line should be a sincere appreciation and a genuine "thank you." Everyone wants to know when they have done a good job. That applies across the entire organization. They want to hear it from their boss. They want to hear it from their clients, their staff, and their customers. They want to know that they have had a successful impact. Most of all, they want to know that your comments and any praise are genuine.

So reach out to say something to everyone who has helped make the project work out. Start with those who provide the foundation for success and work at the often "thankless" everyday tasks. Be sure to thank administrative staff, the mailroom, clerks, cleaning crews, and anyone who too often might be overlooked.

Don't make the mistake of withholding praise, up or down the line. Don't keep it for a select few. Spread the word and say "thank you." While for some sharing praise can be difficult, it is so very important. Your reputation and the reputation of the enterprise will feel the benefit.

Eight Steps to Engaged Action

Every business effort has well-defined and very specific goals. It is vital that you make the extra effort to explain those goals to everyone involved and how you plan to allocate resources to reach those goals. Your success will depend in great measure on your skill in communicating this information so that you can motivate and engage people, build common understandings, and identify shared objectives.

Whether the goal is to earn a return for private business owners, do good works on behalf of people in need, meet the financial-market dividend expected by public shareholders, or lobby on behalf of constituents who believe strongly in one cause or another, you need to communicate with and engage those who are vital to your success. They must be kept informed at each stage in the process and understand your motivation and purpose. They may well be the source of insights, new ideas, and support. Engagement with them is essential.

In my experience, the following Eight Steps to Engagement can ensure that your decisions and communications help you engage effectively and successfully.

Step 1—Research facts and opinions.

Step 2—Engage with those who matter and listen to their views.

Step 3—Decide what to do.

Step 4—Communicate your decision.

Step 5—Act/Behave/Implement your decision.

Step 6—Communicate again—what you did and why.

Step 7—Engage again and listen to reactions—get feedback.

Step 8—Evaluate and plan for next steps.

These eight steps are part of a process and each one is vital. They are most effective when they build on one another. They encompass a thought and listening process so that your decisions are sound and understood and encourage commitment. Moreover, because the process means you go back and ask for reactions and feedback, it is clear to everyone involved that you want input because you recognize that you may well need to change or modify what has been done at some point along the way. In short, you respect the views of others and you want to hear what they think.

STEP 1—RESEARCH FACTS AND OPINIONS

There can be no effective communications on important issues without a foundation in research. You need to ask the tough questions and get answers so that you have an understanding about the perceptions that are held by those who are important to your success. You need to know their views, their positions, and their expectations . . . before you act.

Virtually every organization conducts research of some kind or another. Call it what they will, they may do market studies, focus groups, surveys, original research, or use secondary sources. Research may be formal and conducted by a professional research firm or it may be informal, such as sitting down for one-on-one meetings with key stakeholders, clients, or customers.

Key to galvanizing others and reaching a common decision is a clear, objective assessment of the facts. The important questions then become: What are the key facts we need to consider? What perceptions or opinions need to be factored into our decision? What role does reputation play? Will our actions be in concert with words? Will we be seen as credible?

Listen to what you hear. There may be some very important clues that will make the difference between success and failure.

STEP 2—ENGAGE WITH THOSE WHO MATTER AND LISTEN TO THEIR VIEWS

Engagement is vital from the very start. Talk informally and in a very personal way with those who make it possible for you to succeed. Sit down with them in as individual and personal a way as possible.

For example, if you work in a nonprofit public healthcare facility, take the time to walk and talk with patients and, equally important, patient families.

If you work with a charity, make a point of visiting those to whom you give. Also sit down with donors. Talk with them about why they decide to give to your organization, what additional initiatives they would like to see taken, and ask what would encourage them to contribute even more.

If you are with a consumer products company, go to the customers and interact with them. Ask their opinions on the quality of products and service levels. Ask about the customer service process and how they feel when they call the company. Learn if they believe your claims about your product. Walk the floors of the store and talk with shoppers in the aisles. Work the cash register. Sit down at the kitchen table with moms and dads and listen to praise, criticisms, and reactions.

This kind of engagement is very personal. It is not the same as a formal survey or market study yet it might be just as powerful, or even more so. It is the chance to talk face-to-face with people who matter the most to your organization.

Create those opportunities to engage in a dialog. What you're told can be vital to success.

STEP 3—DECIDE WHAT TO DO

You've researched. You've listened. There is input from those you respect and value. The best available information is in hand. You're now prepared. Make the decision.

STEP 4—COMMUNICATE YOUR DECISION

Announcing your decision is your first communication step. Essentially, it is the opportunity to "say what you are going to do" before you do it. You are outlining what is going to happen. In the process, you will likely get additional feedback. Perhaps there are factors you didn't initially consider that might be uncovered now, before you have actually put the plan in motion.

This is also a key time to explain why the action you are taking is the right one for your organization. This step gives you a chance to talk about how the decision supports the organization's values, how you came to your decision, what results the organization can expect to receive, and what you think is important. It also gives you the opportunity to gauge how your decision will likely be received.

Keep in mind that this is an important opportunity to ask yourself whether your plan fully takes into consideration all the feedback you have received. If it does, move forward. If it does not, make any final corrections.

STEP 5—ACT/BEHAVE/IMPLEMENT YOUR DECISION

Now is the time for action. You have made your decision. You received feedback and factored it into your decision. It's time to act and put plans into motion.

STEP 6—COMMUNICATE AGAIN—WHAT YOU DID AND WHY

You are ready to communicate what you have done and, once again, explain your decision. Before, they heard what you were planning. Then they saw you do it. And now they are hearing you talk about what you did, why you did it, and the results to be expected. It is the moment to put everything into context.

STEP 7—ENGAGE AGAIN AND LISTEN TO REACTIONS—GET FEEDBACK

Feedback will come quite quickly. Some people will support the steps you took. Others may criticize. This is the opportunity to engage in discussions so that you have the value of others' opinions after your decision has been implemented and they can gauge the results. They will want to know several things: Did you do what you said you would do? Did your actions mirror your words and your values? Did you demonstrate caring for others and for the organization? Were you fair?

STEP 8—EVALUATE AND PLAN FOR NEXT STEPS

Be eager to look back and evaluate how things went . . . all with a view to doing things better the next time. This is the moment for reflection, evaluation, and candor.

These Eight Steps to Engagement are simply a guide. To follow them exactly is not the main point. What does matter is that if you want to build a successful career, you need to understand how important engagement is. Give people a thought process to follow to reach your common objectives.

You may do this instinctively. But it is a good idea to do it consciously, and more often. Create a checklist and follow a process for collecting information, sharing it with those whose support is needed, gathering feedback, refining messages, ultimately acting, and then evaluating.

The key to all of this is the determination to engage others and then act. When they are fully on board with what you're doing, and you accomplish it, you have just taken an important step toward a strong and positive reputation. Engagement is that powerful. When engagement is coupled with a personal touch, every interaction can be a pleasure.

People enjoy working with people they believe are genuine and not afraid of showing who they really are. That's why the next chapter is all about being personal.

chapter

Be Personal

The key to me is an intense personal involvement, regardless of the time of day or night and regardless of what else is going on. Clients feel that. They react positively. And, when they are asked about their professional relationship, they always describe it in personal terms.
—Gary Schpero, former law partner at Simpson Thacher & Bartlett

WE HAVE INSTINCTIVE reactions when we meet and speak with others. We usually can tell if someone with whom we might do business actually cares and is likely to take very personally any commitments he makes to us. It's almost as if we can hear it in the voice. And we can certainly see it in the eyes.

To some, this might sound rather corny but it is true.

Think about the number of times you have dealt with someone when trying to ask a question or get more information. Or think about your last discussion with a customer service representative.

Whether you call on the phone or walk into a bank or a retail store, you most often can quickly sense whether the person you're dealing with sees the position as just a job, and is simply going through the motions, or genuinely takes the responsibility personally.

What's your reaction when the customer service representative says, "I am sorry for the problem you are facing"? That is the telltale moment. Do you hear those words as genuine? Or do you hear those words only as a way of trying to disarm you, rather than addressing the problem?

The truth is that two people can say those words and the perceptions will be quite different. On the one hand, it could well be a very sincere apology because the person really is proud of the product or service. On the other hand, it could just be a few words the employee has been taught to say and is now using in the hope they will cover up the fact that he or she can't or doesn't really want to do anything about your concern.

Regardless, the tone, style, and manner in which those words are spoken can often tell much more about sincerity and personal commitment than do the words themselves. Think about it. We are all different. But how you would like others to sound and behave in dealing with you is exactly the way you should sound and behave yourself.

Being personally involved is key and it means thinking about how others will perceive your words and actions.

As Bill Segal—entrepreneur, small business owner, and real estate attorney in South Florida—puts it:

> Is there any distinction between my personal reputation and that of my business? None whatsoever. They must be identical. Both must be genuine and proven by actions. This is especially so in the case of a small business where at the outset you are manager, boss, and key employee, all rolled into one.

Reputations Are Both Personal and Professional

Leslie Gaines-Ross, chief reputation strategist at global communications firm Weber Shandwick, has this to say.

> When I first began my quest to better understand what drives reputation, I approached the topic more clinically—as something that applied exclusively to a specific group of senior professionals and less to me personally. But over time, I came to realize that reputation is personal and it applies to each one of us at work, at home, with friends, and within our community.

When it comes to your reputation and long-term success, there's one thing that we can say for sure: *It's all very personal.* It's personal when it is your reputation as an individual. And it's personal when it is your professional reputation and relates to those around you and to the organization where you work.

The two are linked . . . inextricably.

You cannot separate your individual and your professional reputation. Your reputation follows you every day. There really is no difference between what is personal and what is your professional reputation.

When it comes to building strong connections in the workplace, experienced and successful people relate to the people they work with in ways that are very personal. They make a point of knowing each other well. They speak in personal terms, not in "organizational speak." They look to reach out in a way that recognizes that everyone on the team is a unique person with something to offer. They are eager to build relationships among team members in which everyone feels a bond.

Gary Schpero has a very unique perspective that bridges the importance of the manager's team with client needs. Schpero explains:

> I knew that I had to reach out on a personal level. It wasn't enough that I was a member of law firm this or that. Clients look to each of us very personally. Of course, they need to believe that we have the best skills but, even more important, they need to feel that we care and that we will always think of them first.

> To me, that personal commitment was "palpable." The client knew that I was engaged deeply with them, had high expectations, and never wanted to let my client down.

> As I look at it now, it never was only the law. In fact, I never came anywhere close to believing that I had an understanding of the law that was better than anyone else. Of course, I was well trained but even that wasn't it. Rather, it was my focus on communicating forthrightly with my clients and my commitment to what I saw as a personal commitment, therefore personal relationship, with each.

Commitment and personal dedication can be shown in many ways. It might be the extra attention you pay to helping a colleague, a customer, or a client by making sure that they get the very best service. Or it might be the time and care you take to help others with their careers. Or it might be the extra things that you do to reach out in a personal way, such as cards on special days, inviting them to join you for dinner, or notes of congratulations on important milestones at work or in the family. Or it might be the care you take to make sure a customer has the benefit of that extra effort or thought when it could make a difference.

I recall a colleague who was beloved by his client, a product manager. The company had announced a product recall late one afternoon and it was clear that the next morning the media—print and online—would be running with a series of critical stories. The client and the company had been proactive, announcing the recall themselves and making themselves available to the media, answering questions and distributing a press release, a question-and-answer document, and sharing the background of the product and the reason for the recall. Regardless of the steps that had been taken, it was essential to anticipate that the media would be aggressive. After all, bad news sells and sensational headlines attract eyeballs.

My colleague knew that the online stories would be posted shortly after midnight and that the early morning edition newspapers would have the story on newsstands before the sun came up.

So what did he do that demonstrated his personal commitment so dramatically? Without missing a beat, he was up almost all night on the Internet to read the stories and send them to his client. And then he was at the local newsstand to get the first copies of the paper right off the truck when the early editions were first delivered. By 7:00 in the morning, he had prepared both a report and an analysis of the media coverage so that his client could brief his superiors, decide on next steps, and address the concerns that had been raised.

What did that mean to the client himself and to the company? It meant that there were no surprises. The client could brief his management and plan for the day. There was no question that the client knew and felt the commitment. My colleague had gone out of his way to do what he would have wanted someone else to do for him if he were in the product manager's position. And he did it without even being asked.

Moreover, he put the client in a stronger position. In spite of media coverage that was critical, he helped him be prepared, know and analyze what had been said, and, most important, be ready for the next phase of media coverage.

This was a real partner. This was a colleague who knew the value and importance of personal commitment. And so did his client. This kind of intense commitment you could see, hear, and feel. It was real.

A Word of Caution

Blending the personal and the professional is important but it can be a challenge. The way many people view business is that it is to be hard-nosed, impassionate, and often impersonal. Perhaps this is a natural focus because the primary goal of business is to earn a return for its investors. It implies that there may be little room for things personal.

Just remember what the late Milton Friedman wrote in *New York Times Magazine* in his now-famous article of September 13, 1970, titled "The Social Responsibility of Business is to Increase Profits." Friedman, an economist, clearly placed money as the singular focus of the business. In that seminal article, he wrote:

> In a free-enterprise, private property system, a corporate executive is an employee of the owners of the business. He has direct responsibility to his employers. That responsibility is to conduct the business in accordance with their desires, which generally will be to make as much money as possible while conforming to the basic rules of society, both those embodied in law and those embodied in ethical custom.

If we think about it, though, even a strident view like that of Friedman doesn't mean that we don't behave as individuals and react in personal ways. In fact, you could argue that blending the personal with the professional is, in fact, a way of making the business even more successful, thereby meeting all the goals of business, including the financial ones.

I would argue just that, and therefore, there must be a blend.

The challenge then becomes ensuring that there is nothing improper in the way the personal and the professional blend. And that appears to be difficult in today's world, especially against a backdrop of so many headlines critical of businesses, executives, and both personal and business decisions. Sadly, it makes for too frequent criticism when we perceive that the blend is for personal gain or justification for behavior that is improper.

In short, the proper blend works wonders. The improper blend ruins reputations.

So when is the boundary between the personal and the professional crossed? It depends on two things: first, the motive; second, not what you gain but rather what you give up.

In order to determine where you are on that boundary line, you need to ensure that your motive is both respectful to the people with whom you work and hasn't tempted you to abandon any of the values that you hold dear. In other words, be respectful to others, don't take advantage of them, and ensure that everyone comes out a winner. And stay firm, ensuring that your actions don't run counter to the values that underscore your reputation for doing what is right.

If that boundary is crossed, it is unprofessional and your reputation will suffer. As we have seen too often, that will serve as the end of a promising career or the fall from grace of an otherwise accomplished professional. There have been plenty of the latter in the history of business.

Don't let that happen to you. Blend the personal and professional . . . but don't cross the boundary.

Some Appropriate Ways to Demonstrate a Personal Approach

So what are some of the very basic things you can do to communicate a genuine personal commitment to those with whom you work?

Here are some ideas:

▮ Remember the importance of a smile. Nothing else is quite as powerful.

▮ Shake hands . . . it is a wonderful, personal greeting and a gesture that communicates openness, friendship, and immediate understanding.

▮ Don't forget, only firm handshakes make the grade.

❙ And look them in the eyes when you shake hands … nothing communicates sincerity like direct contact, eye-to-eye.

❙ Remember important dates and reach out to those who have been part of your success. Celebrate your team.

❙ Send congratulatory notes or flowers on key employee anniversaries.

❙ Know those you are meeting. Learn something about them in advance: hobbies, interests, families. Or tell a story that brings people together.

❙ Reach out in times of challenge. If someone working for you is faced with a family or personal challenge, is there something you could do? At least ask.

❙ Send a handwritten note ... there is no more powerful way to say "thank you" or "congratulations."

❙ Walk the halls to say hello.

❙ Talk about your family and your interests ... it opens the doors so that others feel comfortable sharing their news.

❙ Put whatever you say in a context that relates to those around you.

❙ Look at everyone as if each person is your best friend, mentor, and champion.

❙ Do something unexpected ... a small gift for a special success, or just a thank-you note.

Most important, go out of your way. Do more than you are asked to do. Go two steps farther than any others would do. It will be noticed. Your reputation will climb and your career will too.

So is any of this really important? Absolutely. It is an essential component of success.

The Personal Touch in Business Practices

Manny and Lily Dominguez, husband and wife, own and manage a neighborhood pharmacy in New Jersey. They explain how a distinctively personal touch helped them get started and now keeps them successful:

> Our values are "trust," "a family pharmacy," and a "personal environment." We do some very special things so that we can create that kind of feeling. Most patients need some sort of guidance. When they have questions, we take the time to talk with them. In fact, we actually set aside a small office so that we can consult with our patients in an environment that is private and personal. Rather than talking to patients about their health concerns while standing in the aisles or at the open counter, we wanted to make them comfortable, avoid any embarrassment, and give them the chance to talk. It is a room with a desk and chairs, right off the pharmacy area, for private conversations and consultations. We also do a number of other things to put the patient at ease. They can sit down, talk with us, and, if they have concerns about blood pressure, blood sugar, filling out insurance forms, or just understanding their medications, we can sit with them and help. Because we know this is so important to our patients, we hired a specialist who is there simply to help with these kinds of things.

If we think about the special approach that the Dominguez family has taken in building their business, there are some clear signals that they understand their customers and have built their pharmacy around a mission of meeting their customers'—or as they call them, their patients'—needs. The result is a comfortable environment for their patients—one in which they can share their concerns and fears. That personal approach and personal environment keeps them coming back. This is a powerful strategy and one that has built a reputation for caring and personal attention. And it is genuine.

Each of us has the opportunity to create a similar reputation for ourselves and, thereby, build our careers.

"How" Is More Important than "What"

In any kind of business, a personal approach can prove to be the key factor in making a sale and earning the trust of a customer or a client. Over the years, I have had the opportunity to work with clients as they made decisions about retaining a range of advisers and outside consultants. In some cases, I have participated in the evaluations. And, in other cases, I have helped develop the criteria for making the final decision.

Experience has shown that many organizations tend to get caught up in the idea of a formal proposal and focus most of their attention in that area. No doubt credentials, the proposed team, and preliminary ideas and recommendations are important. Yet, there are many applicants who have similar experience, are staffed with well-qualified teams of professionals, and are well equipped to recommend sound ideas.

If you cut to the chase and ask what the differentiating factor is, some will describe it as "chemistry" and others will describe it as a "personal connection." How do you know if the chemistry or that personal connection is right?

The answer is simply that it is a sense of personal commitment that comes across and resonates with each of us. That often will prove to be the critical factor and will win your business.

I remember one situation in particular when I was a member of a selection committee. The field of potential advisers had been narrowed down to three teams. Each of the teams had provided their credentials in writing and had sent in their early thinking. That meant the written part of the process had been completed.

The first two teams were okay. Nothing stood out. They were all more than qualified and said the right things.

But the third team was different . . . right from the start. It was the way they walked into the board room—the enthusiasm. They took the time to walk the room, shaking everyone's hand, confident, smiling, and introducing themselves. When they went to the head of the table, you couldn't help but notice that they were looking directly at everyone and eager to start. In fact, the more senior adviser never sat down. She remained standing through the formal introductions and then started the presentation. She talked from personal knowledge about the experience and qualities of each member of her team as she introduced them. You knew it wasn't just a formal bio memorized. She looked at each of us as she spoke. And her opening comments clearly demonstrated how much research the team had done about our group. She stressed some of the unique qualities of our organization—our history and, importantly, our values—and dove right in on strategy, followed by how she would expect her team to be evaluated on performance.

From the outset, you knew the team cared. Yes, they were good at making presentations. No doubt. But you also knew they had taken the time to think through in detail what they would say and the conviction with which they would say it. In other words, they cared enough to rehearse often—like focused athletes, practicing well before the big game—and to make sure that what they had to say was direct, simple, and relevant. Those attributes are especially important because you can't be direct, simple, and relevant if you haven't done your homework and focused your thoughts.

From the very beginning, the tone in their voices, their candor, the research, the way they looked directly at you, the ideas they shared, and the emotion they conveyed when they asked for the business were impressive.

Hands down, that third team emerged the victor and the relationship has lasted years.

Once again, as in many aspects of building your reputation, the lesson is that it is not only what you do or say that is important, but also how you do it and say it.

The fact is, when you listen carefully, you can tell very quickly if the personal commitment is there. We could see it. We could hear it. In fact, we could feel it.

In the same situation, you would too.

One of the key takeaways from this example is that those who are most thoughtful and eager will approach an assignment with a balance of fact and emotion . . . a balance of the business and the personal. Of course, there will be detailed research and candid recommendations. Moreover, regardless of how cold and calculated the facts may be, the discussion itself will be one in which there are some very clear signals of a strong personal connection. The tone will, of course, be respectful and one that communicates a genuine caring for you, your organization, and how important the opportunity to do the work actually is. And there will be some very clear moments when you can sense the personal commitment.

The "How" of Standing Apart and Getting Hired

When it comes to landing the client or getting hired by a company, there are four hows of communicating personal commitment.

I *How do you say it?* Do you speak with conviction? Do you convey a sense of passion for the issues being addressed? Do you relate the potential assignment to the values of the organization and what it holds important? Do you really care . . . or is it just an act?

I *How do you behave?* Do you reach out to people individually? Do you walk directly to them with confidence to greet them and introduce yourself? Have you done your homework about each of the people in the room, and do you look at them when they speak? Are you relaxed and confident? Are you being genuine? Are your words and behavior in sync?

I *How do they react?* Your success depends on their reaction. Do they believe what you are saying? They will be wondering whether they would like to work with your team and, especially, with you. Do you convey that they are an important priority for you?

I *How do they feel?* People will be judging you by their gut reaction as much as anything. Do you look directly at them? When you make a commitment, do they feel you really are committed? How can you make them feel that you will be ready, willing, and able at any time to help them?

Most often the "how" will win out over the "what." Many are qualified to execute the "what" on a potential client's or employer's behalf. But very few will stand out if judged by the "how." In the long run, the relationships that will be the strongest, those that will endure and last the longest, will be based on the "how": the personal commitment.

The simple fact is that strong relationships—those with a strong personal connection—can overcome mistakes and problems, but weak relationships cannot tolerate even the simplest mistake or problem. And we all know that, at some time in any relationship, mistakes and problems will arise. This kind of personal commitment is the stuff of strong reputations that endure and careers that grow.

Examples of the Personal Touch

The importance of the personal touch resonates among many distinguished and accomplished professionals. For them, it has proven to be an important element of success. Throughout this book—both in chapters already read and in those yet to be read—there are examples of just this.

If we think about Louis Ciolino, we realize he did some very simple things. It started with knowing his customers.

If we think of establishing a gallery in the office to showcase employee art, we see that it is a very simple concept. It starts with recognizing that each one of us has a personal life and individual interests.

As David Fox says in another chapter, he put his own reputation on the line in dealing with a crisis. That single act speaks loudly to us about personal commitment.

If we think of the private consultation room in the Dominguez pharmacy, we understand that the owners struck a chord to make their patients feel "safe." They knew that talking about personal problems is never comfortable in a public area.

When we think about taking the time to provide career feedback in both formal and informal ways, we see that it demonstrates caring for the growth of those who work with us and a personal interest in their careers.

If we think about Gary Schpero's belief that personal commitment must be "palpable," we see commitment that business colleagues need to see and feel.

As Ted Athanassiades shares in a later chapter, it is his intense focus on listening to colleagues that says a lot about learning from others and the power of the personal approach.

If we think about Steve Joenk sweeping the floor in his shirt and tie, we hear a message of personal dedication.

If we think of the fact that Harvey Rosenthal would carve out time to go back to the Swampscott store during Christmas time, we learn about taking things personally.

When we think about walking the halls to say hello and chat with staff, we see that it shows we are individuals who care about each other. No one is to be taken for granted.

If we think about what Bill Kearns says about being personal, looking others in the eye and telling them what is real, it reinforces the principles of candor and honesty.

When we recall what Rose Mann says about treating everyone with respect and kindness, we learn not to be judgmental.

If we think about sharing praise, we realize there is nothing more personal or meaningful than a simple "thank you" for a job well done. Even without the baseballs, "thank you" goes a very long way.

When we think about what Jettie Edwards says about the need for candor and confidence, we see a facet of relationships that is essential to doing a job well.

These are all different ways of making personal statements. Some may think they are not essential, but those people are wrong. Others would argue that they are not the hard stuff of business, but they too are wrong.

These personal approaches most definitely are essential. They make a difference. They demonstrate the power of an approach that, to so many, means caring, support, encouragement, and honesty.

In short, they build the kind of reputation that leads to success. They help build the most valuable asset in any genuine working relationship: trust.

The next part of this book is about just that—how to build and defend trust, and how to make it long lasting.

part three

trust

Trust is at the root of any economic system based on mutually beneficial exchange. In virtually all transactions, we rely on the word of those with whom we do business. . . . If a significant number of business people violated the trust upon which our interactions are based, our court system and our economy would be swamped into immobility.

—Alan Greenspan, retired chairman of the Board of
Governors of the Federal Reserve System of the United States[1]

The Internet start-up craze of the late 1990s was followed by crashes, bankruptcies, and failures. By the beginning of the next decade, it was clear that the devastating financial impact extended well beyond the doors of the start-up companies to organizations that had put their faith in the potential that those companies represented. Too much came too fast...and too many promises were fueled by an excitement that didn't match reality.

The dot-com era opened up new opportunities by testing both the boundaries of the information age and the development of the technology that dramatically changed the way people communicate and gain access to information. However, it also provided testimony to the need for trust in business.

Funding for start-up Internet companies came fast and furious. Venture capital firms saw an opportunity to get in at the ground floor of an industry with potentially large growth opportunities. The excitement continued, spurned by marketing dollars, but the revenue didn't follow.

Financial results disappointed many. People questioned their decisions to invest in these companies once they realized the dot-coms were not delivering the results they imagined. Trust diminished. Confidence plummeted. The bloom was off the rose.

There were few organizations that escaped the impact when those Internet companies shuttered their doors and left their strategic partners and suppliers hanging. Some felt it more so than others. In the firm I managed, we were fortunate. We had smart managers who were cautious and prepared for a possible downturn because they knew how important it was to be able to make the right decisions at the first stages of a client relationship, even when the financial pressures might encourage others to behave differently. They knew that the reputation of the firm depended on a balance between stability and informed risk-taking. Ultimately, they knew that the mandate was to do the right thing . . . regardless.

During that period, our managers would have numerous meetings trying to determine whether we would get paid for the work already done. As a consulting firm, our receivables were always more than thirty days out, but in good economic times we were paid promptly. Not so in this collapse. As a result, our financial and legal teams often had to visit the client to negotiate what could and should be done regarding payment.

In those discussions, I knew there would be questions of judgment when it came to reaching a settlement. In some cases we would prevail. In other cases we simply needed to take the loss, write off the invoices, and move on. I left those decisions to the managers doing the negotiations. Whatever the team did, I was confident that the values we shaped for the firm—and our reputation as a responsible organization—would serve us well.

One of the most rewarding compliments I have ever received came during those challenging times from Linda Hersh, an extraordinarily talented member of our legal team whose every assignment demonstrated great character and values. At the end of a series of negotiations with a client to resolve an overdue receivable—and in her wonderful style of being straightforward, succinct, and to the point—she simply said, "Thank you for creating the environment where we could 'do the right thing.'"

In an environment of earned trust, in which everyone is expected to do the right thing, our employees rose to the occasion and fulfilled our mandate of integrity.

NOTE

1. Remarks by Chairman Alan Greenspan, published by The Federal Reserve Board. Accessed at www.federalreserve.gov/boarddocs/speeches/1999/199906102.htm.

chapter 10

Build a Circle of Trust

Reputation is the basis of leadership, no matter the job. It is a reflection of your character, your integrity and, in so many ways, your caring for those who work with you. But trust is only built over time, based on how you handle all types of situations, good and bad. It is also reflected in our personal lives. Simply put, trust is a product of our choices, both individual and professional.

— David Fox, retired chairman and chief executive of Northern Trust Company

THE MOST COMMONLY voiced definition of reputation is that it is how we are seen by others. That being the case, the critical question then becomes, "On what do they base how they see us?" The quick answer is "our actions—or the way we behave." But that may be rather simplistic.

The fact is, when people make judgments about you or me, they look at a number of factors. Most often, they want to know more about how and why we make our decisions and, ultimately, how and why we do the things we do. Importantly, they also want to know if what they saw in the past will be what they can expect in the future.

One quality that is woven deeply into the fabric of these questions is the concept of trust. Simply put, trust stands at the center of the vortex when it comes to our reputation . . . and, therefore, how we are seen.

In our personal lives, we instinctively recognize the inextricable link between trust and reputation. We know that a lack of trust leads to a bad reputation and the presence of trust leads to a strong reputation. You can't have one without the other. The link between trust and reputation is what defines all of our personal relationships.

This concept is so fundamental to our daily lives that we often don't even think about it. It is symbolized every time we shake another's hand and voice any sort of commitment. It is the basis on which we buy and sell, qualify for and use a credit card, or obtain a home mortgage. It is the basis for how we relate to our neighbors, to people in our community and our schools, and to local and national political leaders. And it is a guiding principle in how we raise our children and teach them the qualities they will need for success in both their personal and professional relationships.

To me, trust is a wonderful and very powerful word. It is almost magical. It is laden with emotion. Everyone seems to know what trust means. They immediately sense all the connotations. Volumes have been written about trust—how it has shaped the outcome of world events and how the lack of it has, at times, changed the world. Lyrics for popular music, opera, and the stage are about trust—trust honored, trust shattered. Tributes and honors praise the trustworthy. And politicians rue the day they lost their constituents' trust.

A trusting relationship is so much a part of our history and culture that it is personified by Norman Rockwell's images of daily life in America, whether families at a meal, kids together, or the classic painting of a lunch-eonette soda fountain where a policeman and a young boy lean toward each other, an unspoken bond between them as they sit side-by-side.

In our professional lives, regardless of the type of organization where we work, trust is the defining element of our relationships. It underlies everything about the way we work and how we relate to those around us. Without trust, everything in our free enterprise society would come to a halt.

Alan Greenspan saw the impact of trust very clearly. An economist by training, he put it succinctly when he spoke these words of caution to Harvard University graduates in his commencement address on June 10, 1999:

> Your success in life, and the success of our country, is going to depend on the integrity and other qualities of character that you and

your contemporaries will continue to develop and demonstrate over the years ahead. A generation from now, as you watch your children graduate, you will want to be able to say that whatever success you achieved was the result of honest and productive work, and that you dealt with people the way you would want them to deal with you.

Civilization, our civilization, rests on that premise.

I cannot speak for others whose psyches I may not be able to comprehend, but, in my working life, I have found no greater satisfaction than achieving success through honest dealings and strict adherence to the view that for you to gain, those you deal with should gain as well. Human relations—be they personal or professional—should not be zero sum gains.[1]

Trust in Yourself and Others

Even in the toughest of work environments, at the core of a strong reputation is the confidence to believe in yourself, in your judgment of others, and in what will be best for the team.

The simple fact is that before you can be a successful manager with the kind of reputation that encourages others to follow you and trust your judgment, you need to believe in and trust yourself. That is the first step. Believe in yourself and you will have the self-confidence to believe in others. Trust yourself and you will trust others.

Trusting others is so important. When you do, those you trust most often live up to expectations. With time, they too trust themselves and, in turn, also have the self-confidence to trust others. And so the pattern repeats itself.

This is one of the most critical lessons when it comes to reputation and for understanding what it takes to be confident enough to share your reputation with others and your team.

The Circle of Reputation

Rarely is a businessperson's reputation due solely to what he or she accomplishes alone. In fact, I would venture to say that most people cannot accomplish very much on their own. Unless you are Robinson Crusoe on a deserted island—and eventually even he had help from Friday—we all need to be part of a team and have others help us by doing their part so that we can reach our goals and live up to our potential.

Organizations of all types—nonprofit, trade associations, public service, or business—are built around a structure that requires people to work together, all pulling in the same direction to reach specific goals. The teams that work best are those in which each person has self-confidence. That creates a strong partnership culture. They are united in purpose. They have defined leadership. They have a diverse range of talents. And they have members who have been selected because they bring complementary skills and resources. Together, they constitute a team, often stronger when working together than working individually.

To be sure, in order to be part of a team, you have to give something up. You give something up to get something more in return. You give up some of your independence, your authority, and some of your ego to receive the benefits that flow from a team effort.

None of this diminishes your efforts, your contribution, or the credit you deserve. In fact, it is often said that, in life, you get more than you give.

When you have the self-confidence to share power and authority, your reputation is enhanced. Your fellow team members see you as someone who appreciates them and, in turn, they work harder. They believe in you and they are confident that your goals and theirs are one and the same. This empowers them. The accomplishments, they know, will accrue to everyone on the team. They are not concerned about working hard and not being appreciated. Quite the contrary, they know they are valued. They know they are part of the circle of reputation.

John Maltese, now retired from his role as a chief financial officer, is well trained in financial management and has what we all think of as "street smarts." He led a worldwide financial management team, working to strengthen financial controls and increase the bottom line. When it comes to building a circle of trust, he puts it this way:

> Reputation is built over many years, one step at a time. In the beginning, if you are eager and a hard worker, your reputation will be just that: a "go-getter," "smart," and "works hard." But that only goes so far. The fact is, unless you work for someone who is confident and able to give credit when credit is due, you may go unnoticed for

a long time. If that happens, whatever reputation you've been building for yourself will just die on the vine.

Because of that simple fact, I believe a strong manager—with a strong reputation—has the obligation to share his or her reputation. That might sound strange, especially using the word "share" when it comes to reputation.

I'm just a simple guy and I look at it this way. If my reputation is based on whether or not others trust me, then, in turn, I need to be able to trust those who work for me. When I do, in effect, I am sharing the trust in me with them. My logic is simple: if others trust me—and I trust those who work for me—then those who trust me will trust the people who work for me.

I came from an environment where, in the beginning of my career, I did every job myself: an analysis, a reconciliation, a report, or a financial statement.

As I became more and more skilled at managing others, my confidence grew. But I never forgot to share my reputation with those who deserved it. I trusted them so we became much stronger as a team. The team, in turn, took on the same reputation.

So, if I put all of it together, the most important lessons that I learned are three:

First, you must believe in those who work with you on your team.

Second, manage them in a way that fosters the best work possible and, when they perform, heap praise on them.

And third, share your reputation with them if they deserve it by trusting them as others trust you.

Strong Leaders Share Power

To be successful, there is an especially delicate balance that you must reach. On one hand, you need to be the leader, to stand out, and be sure to move projects and the organization in the right direction, reaching your objectives.

On the other hand, to be effective for the organization in the long run, you must find a way to share both the challenges and the successes with your team and, in the process, build a sense of partnership.

Some find this to be a hard balance to strike.

It is easy to understand why. Those who become leaders generally tend to have strong traits. Most often they are promoted based on a track record that has demonstrated their enthusiasm and eagerness to take charge, make decisions, or provide direct guidance. Once promoted to manager, those same individuals often find it a struggle to step aside, let other team members assume responsibility, and, when the assignment is completed, share the credit.

To do just that, a person in a leadership role needs to be willing to relinquish some power. That can be threatening. For some, sharing power and authority is one of the most difficult tasks on earth—if not an impossible one. Others may decide to give up power, but only reluctantly and then only when they believe they have no other choice. And of course, there are those who simply refuse outright and never budge. Perhaps it is ego. Or maybe fear just takes over.

Yet, sharing power is an essential skill possessed by the most experienced managers who realize the value of their reputation. They see sharing as a strength, not a weakness, and as a dynamic force for genuine leadership and for serving the organization best over the long haul.

However, the question remains: How to ensure that even the most driven businesspeople put ego aside to focus on the organization and the team?

In my experience, the challenge is best described as finding a path between two quotes, one of which is among my favorites and the other among the most interesting.

The first appeared in a newspaper many years ago. There was an ad with the headline "You can't get off the ground without the pilot." I've had those words—the newspaper clipping—framed in my office for as long as I can remember. It's not because I was a combat helicopter pilot but rather because those nine words reveal so much about leadership: someone needs to make the final decision and lift the airplane off the ground . . . or it goes nowhere.

The second quote challenges us to think deeply: "It is not who is right, but what is right, that is of importance." The words are from nineteenth-century British biologist Thomas Huxley.

If you merge the messages of those two quotes, the combination emphasizes that leaders, although aware of their important role, need to remember that what counts is not that they are right but that the team does the right thing. Interestingly, none of this diminishes the leader's role, nor does it undermine his or her importance. Quite the contrary. It bolsters the leader's reputation as a strong, confident, and considerate leader who has the right priority and the right focus.

David Fox talks in very frank terms about how reputation and trust must have roots that are strong and deep.

He talks about leadership and sharing power with a team. He speaks forcefully about his belief that a strong sense of trust must be visible and come alive, with credit for success going to everyone involved, not just the leader:

> I tell everyone that I got my MBA at the University of Chicago but I got my real graduate education in the Marine Corps. I don't know of any other event in my life that has helped as much to form my management style as my experience as an officer in the Marine Corps.
>
> If ever there were a lesson about trust, it comes from the military.
>
> One of the biggest challenges I faced at Northern Trust was in the 1980s when many of our loans for oil and gas exploration ran into problems and the borrowers defaulted. It probably was one of the most difficult times of my career, because Northern's reputation for conservative lending was called into question. Since Commercial Banking reported to me, it was my responsibility to form a team to clean up the problems, find out what went wrong, and ensure it never happened again. Who would be on that team and how we would operate were critical. As in the Marine Corps, we needed people who would offer tough questions; unvarnished answers; objective assessments; no gloss on the problems; high integrity; the ability to work across various groups and specialties without regard to territory; no rush to judgments and no taking sides or trying to garner credit. In short, they were chosen based on their reputations for having those characteristics.

Each month, I would report the team's progress and problems directly to the Northern Trust Board of Directors. As you can imagine, these often were very uncomfortable meetings, but we kept the process moving.

Working through the problems and taking our losses was painful and difficult. It took well over two years to work through the many issues involved, and the decisions were tough. Especially as they related to people. Some left the bank but most of the team distinguished themselves and went on to greater responsibilities. And our loan origination and approval process was completely revamped, since we found it to be outdated and at the root of the problem.

The point is that no progress could have been made if there had not been a mutual trust and confidence between the team, its members, and myself. That was especially true on an assignment of this kind, which was critical to our reputation and cut to the core of the values of our bank.

Northern Trust has been around for more than 120 years. Our motto is "Principles That Endure." The real job in the oil and gas crisis was to ensure that those principles did just that... endure.

Steps to Earn Trust

The steps to earning trust involve sharing praise and success for a job well done. That kind of sharing communicates a sense of partnership, support for mutual goals, and respect for everyone's role, regardless of any individual's seniority or stature.

HR World, an online resource and community for human resource professionals, published an article by David Hakala that, in part, urges leaders to behave in a manner that focuses on sharing responsibility and outcomes, not hoarding praise:

Magnanimity means giving credit where it is due. A magnanimous leader ensures that credit for successes is spread as widely as possible throughout the company. Conversely, a good leader takes personal responsibility for failures. This sort of reverse magnanimity helps other people feel good about themselves and draws the team closer together. To spread the fame and take the blame is a hallmark of effective leadership.

Leaders with humility recognize that they are no better or worse than other members of the team. A humble leader is not self-effacing but rather tries to elevate everyone. Leaders with humility also understand that their status does not make them a god.

Openness means being able to listen to new ideas, even if they do not conform to the usual way of thinking. Good leaders are able to suspend judgment while listening to others' ideas, as well as accept new ways of doing things that someone else thought of. Openness builds mutual respect and trust between leaders and followers.[2]

When teamwork, a common bond, and sharing become palatable, they are felt by everyone around. They know they are all in it together...almost like the shout of the nineteenth-century writer Alexandre Dumas's *Three Musketeers* or the legendary declaration of the Swiss Cantons in 1291 when they came together in unity to form the Swiss Confederation: *One for all and all for one.*

Alberto Ibarguen, president and chief executive of the Knight Foundation, shares his experience and heartfelt lessons on gaining trust and the impact of the digital age.

> You will be trusted if those around you believe you are willing to change your mind and embrace new ideas. Nothing has changed our world like the Internet. As a former publisher, I know that first-hand. We have an overload of information and need filters, organizers, and interpreters. In the past, we trusted news organizations to do that. Now, at the beginning of the information revolution, those "I write/you read" structures feel antiquated.
>
> It seems to me that trust is precisely the key element in the rise of social media, with Facebook and Twitter as the prime examples. We look for something that feels somehow more authentic, more real, and find it in the people we know.

The digital age has transformed people from consumers of information to users of information and users of the new media now on everyone's desktop. We still need even newer ideas so that we can ensure that the delivery of information is better and more effective than ever before.

New ideas, honest search for answers, and openness to change . . . those are just some qualities that generate respect and trust.

Earning trust is a never-ending and vital process, especially in a world where skepticism reigns. Here are some tips for how to do it.

I *Learn from those around you.* Each person has a lot to offer. See them as among the most discerning people in the world, with deep experience. Recognize them as professionals whose input is critical to your task. They are intelligent, probing. Don't be quick to rush to judgment and dismiss what they have to say. You likely will learn a lot.

I *Ask the people you work with to be your closest ally and your fiercest critic, all at the same time.* The more open you are with them, the more they will believe that you care and give you their support. If you want their honest opinion and want to hear their views, they will know you trust them. They will live up to the challenge at hand even when the going gets tough.

I *Be open to comments, in-depth questions, and criticism . . . and keep your body language in check.* Don't react negatively, either by word or action, when you hear something you didn't expect or don't agree with. It might be tough at times not to succumb to your instinctive reaction and frown or look away in disdain, but avoid that at all costs. Your open approach to questions demonstrates confidence in yourself and trust in your team.

I *Work from the macro to the micro.* Show your grasp of strategy and the big picture, or macro view. Take the time to lay out and finalize the strategy and long-term goals before you attend to the details—the micro. Be precise and specific. Look at the strategic decision from every direction, both positive and negative.

❙ *Demonstrate your personal commitment.* As every good soldier knows, you lead from up front. Everything you do and say should communicate that you take the first step and you don't ask anyone to do anything you wouldn't do yourself. If you are committed—and clearly communicate your commitment—then the team will be committed too.

❙ *Take the time to fully explain your thinking.* When you pay attention to the details, you can make major inroads into a trusting relationship with the people around you. They will know that you thought about your decisions carefully and, even more important, they will know that you cared enough about them to take the time to provide a complete explanation of your thinking and that you have considered all possibilities. As we tell our children, the more you put into something, the more you will get out of it. People will notice and they will respect you for showing that you respect them.

❙ *Speak from conviction.* Say what you want to say and say it with emotion . . . with feeling. People want to know you are concerned. Why should they go the extra mile by working hard and making sacrifices if you don't? Winning people's trust is very personal. The workplace is not a galley ship with people pulling on oars to the beat of a drum. People are motivated to work their hardest because they believe in you. They respond to your emotion and caring. They don't respond to organizational rhetoric. If they believe in you, they will be committed, both to the strategy and to you.

❙ *Share the leadership role.* Rotate assignments so that others who have proved their potential have the chance and the challenge of taking on necessary high-profile projects. Don't have any preconceived notions. Give them the opportunity to prove themselves.

❙ *Expect nothing but the best.* Clearly lay out your expectations and let everyone rise to their full potential. People can accomplish more than you think. Look for, expect, and reward outstanding performance. More often than not, people will surprise and impress you with their ability.

❙ *Use every bit of the digital technology available to you and use it wisely.* Understand the impact of communication in the digital age. The Internet, blogs, social media, websites, and the dramatic speed with which information and news travels have all had an extraordinary impact on perceptions of trust and, therefore, reputations. Learn to use those techniques.

I *Share trust with those around you.* Trust others and they will trust you.

In short, there is no lasting reputation without a circle of trust among those with whom we deal in our careers. That focus on trust must be reflected each and every day in our words and our actions. If there are inconsistencies—and if we fail to "walk the talk"—those whom we manage and those whose support is vital will notice, and trust will be lost. The result, unfortunately, would be that our goals are not reached and our careers suffer.

Your Personal Intangible Assets

In my MBA studies at the University of Connecticut, Graduate School of Business, we learned quickly that an organization's value is built on both tangible and intangible assets. Textbooks define tangible assets as plants and machinery—resources you can actually touch and those that help manufacture the products sold.

Historically, tangible assets had been the source of an organization's book value. You can count the machines, price the buildings, value the land, and see the raw material being turned into automobiles, clothing, and products destined for showrooms and store shelves. In the past, those tangible assets have also been the primary determinant of a public company's market capital.

As business schools are quick to point out, though, it is the intangible assets—including reputation—that are so crucial and carry a distinct value of their own. The explosive growth of information companies, technology firms, and the service sector has produced valuable assets that you may not be able to physically touch but are, nonetheless, essential and serve as the foundation for valuation. This shift away from manufacturing has put a new face on how we view businesses and the qualities we value most.

Those intangible assets are described as intellectual capital. Intangible assets are not just business school theory and jargon. Of the traditional five intangible assets, three of them directly pertain to what it takes to build a strong reputation:

1. *Human Capital*—The value and knowledge brought to the organization and created by employees.

2. *Relationship Capital*—The sum value of the many people who respect the organization and its leadership so that thought and opinion leaders, such as stakeholders, politicians, regulators, legislators, and the media, can be called upon to voice their thoughts and support the organization.

3. *Reputation Capital*—The intangible asset that represents the organization's residual goodwill in the marketplace that permits support for its endeavors and creates the basis for a second chance if things don't go quite right.

Although those three "assets" most commonly are invoked to refer to corporate or organizational assets, I believe that they are equally relevant to our career "assets"—those qualities that affect our careers and play a very important role in whether or not we will be successful.

When we refer to human capital, it speaks to our selection of those with whom we work or with whom we decide to partner. Selecting them well and building a cadre of talented employees around us who share our values and with whom we communicate openly can make the difference in the insights and intellect that we bring to each task we face.

Relationship capital refers to those whom we can count on to support our initiatives because they respect us and believe that we have the right motivations behind what we want to do.

And reputation capital is all the goodwill we have built up over time based on our earlier decisions and the trust others have in us to do what is right.

These intangible assets—coupled with strong values, doing the right thing, walking the talk, ethical behavior, and being trusted—are essential for our careers and for our long-term success.

Trust in You, Your Products, and Your Company

There is a very close link connecting you, the products or services you provide, and the reputation of the organization where you work. The three are often seen as exactly the same. It is a natural reaction for people to attribute the same qualities and values to all three.

When any of us speaks with someone who sells a product or works in a business, we use the term "you." That term clearly refers not only to the person but also to the product and the organization. There is no distinction. We naturally equate the three. The reason is simple: We personalize organizations and connect them and their products directly to the individuals who are the face of an organization.

Sometimes we even make judgments about the products or the organization based on our perceptions of that individual. Other times we make judgments about the individual based on our perceptions of the product or the organization. Our judgments may or may not be fair and accurate. Regardless, we make those kinds of connections. And again, right or wrong, our expectations follow those perceptions.

Margery Kraus—founder and chief executive of the worldwide consulting firm APCO Worldwide and a recently elected member of the Enterprising Women Hall of Fame—talks about these kinds of perceptions.

> Businesses and trade associations can be much more effective at managing their reputations if they understand how they are perceived by those who matter: employees, investors, public figures, and those in the local community.
>
> And, in much the same way, we can better manage our own organizations when we too focus on our reputation and understand how those closest to us perceive what we do and why we do it. Our own ability to grow and prosper—and be recognized as a leading entrepreneurial organization—has been dependent on our ability to foster a constructive and supportive climate.
>
> Moreover, we understand the critical role that values, trust, and character play in attracting talented people. Our values clearly state this: "tell the truth, empower great people to do great work, nurture an organization where everyone is valued, rely on one another in achieving our personal potential."
>
> The reputation research we do for our clients is clear. People judge behavior, and therefore reputation, based on their expectations. Behavior and expectation are linked. In other words, do what you say and "walk the talk."

With this comes a profound responsibility that each of us bears for our behavior and our values. What we do, how we act, what we say, how we say it . . . all paint a picture for others about us, what we sell, and where we work.

Trust, Values, and the Brand

Richard Edelman, president and chief executive officer of Edelman Worldwide, puts it very simply when talking about individuals and brands: "trust is the key driver." Drawing from the most recent findings of the Edelman Trust Barometer research, he is very pointed in his conclusions when he talks about the importance of trust to success:

> In our study, it was clear that "trust" had become what I called "an essential line of business" for everyone and every business. Now, more than a year later, our Trust Barometer makes it even more clear how important that concept is. Our research continues to show that whether an organization is trusted is critical to its future.
>
> This is a lesson not only for business but also for individuals. For each of us, there can be no long-term success without trust.
>
> Trust, in my view, and, as our research has shown us year after year, is what I call "a protective agent" and leads to tangible benefits. Trust creates the environment where there can be success. At the same time, the corollary is true: lack of trust is a barrier.
>
> From a practical perspective—whether as a business or in our professional careers—this calls for what I describe as a "new trust architecture." We cannot only focus on "what we do," but we also have to focus on "how we do it" and "where we do it." What this means is that, yes, we have to do the "what" of a business—meaning make a profit with purpose and shared values—but we also have to concentrate on "how we do it."

The connection between the "how" and the "what" is critical. We respond to the underlying values of how a business behaves while we watch what that business actually does. The same is true for how we respond to people. This is an important factor in defining reputation—the trust people have in how the organization and its people will behave—and in how we describe the brand.

For some companies the "how" is the driver behind the "what." And the "how" is the driver of the reputation. In those businesses where the founder continues to have a strong role, the culture of "how" things are done is often strongest. The "how" speaks to values and those values play a critical role in the design of products, the nature of the selling process, and how the people who work in the business are selected. In essence, the "how" becomes the brand.

Per Heggenes is CEO of the IKEA Foundation. He has a special perspective on the importance of values and how critical they are to the reputation of a global brand. Widely known for its large bright blue and yellow home-furnishing retail stores, IKEA is a worldwide organization with a very straightforward business idea: "To offer a wide range of well-designed, functional home furnishing products at prices so low that as many people as possible will be able to afford them." With annual sales in excess of 23 billion euros (roughly $33 billion), its success is built on a strong set of values that have shaped how the company does everything.

In my role at the IKEA Foundation, I am acutely aware that the programs we choose to support and the extent of our contributions around the world must be part of an unbroken chain that links together the core values of our retail business, our supply chain partners, the Foundation, our long-term goals, and our founder, Ingvar Kamprad, who started the company more than sixty years ago.

The fact is the core values must be one and the same. Simply put, values make up much of the IKEA brand. They are the fabric of our reputation. They set the standards for how we design and develop products, how we build partnership with our suppliers, how we market our products, and how we treat our customers. Our values make up the good name we have around the world. They are fundamental to our company and to everything we do. As such, they cannot be compromised.

In all of our work at the Foundation, we are committed to a disciplined process that measures funding and program opportunities against a list of well-defined goals and values. Everyone on my team and on my board of directors knows the priorities.

When we look at a range of potential programs, our first step is to evaluate them against a set of key values that apply to everything that IKEA does or is involved with: ethical behavior, quality, long-term partnership, results, accountability, reliability, preservation of the environment, sustainability, renewable energy, reducing carbon footprint, economical packaging, low prices for our customers, constant improvement, and, of course, long-term benefit.

Our second step is to look at potential programs in light of very clear Foundation funding goals. In particular, the actual project must be able to help people change their lives for the better—on a permanent basis. We do that by building strong and lasting partnerships with leading implementing organizations.

As a result, we have focused many of the Foundation giving programs on children, simply because, in our view and given our values, children are the most important people in the world.

I learned early in my career just how powerful a reputation could be if the right values were in place and managers brought them to life each day, in everything they did.

Wherever I go in the world and we put programs into place, I am acutely aware of the IKEA brand and the importance of what is often called "its good name." I also know that I represent the brand. When people talk with me, they look for signs that the IKEA values are strong and credible—and that we actually live those values.

What I have learned is that those values are part of our fabric and our brand. And, because they are strong and apply to all parts of the business, time has proven that they endure. Even after sixty years, they continue to drive a company that provides meaningful, quality products for people, at very reasonable prices. And proceeds from

those sales permit a Foundation to support programs that help
improve opportunities for more than 100 million children.

The IKEA Foundation is a vital part of IKEA's overall reputation. It demonstrates that the company's values are alive and well—and contributing to our world.

Building a circle of trust—based on strong values—creates a reputation that is felt by everyone around you. It permeates your business, your colleagues, your products, those you hire, and those with whom you do business. It becomes the underlying guide for "how" you do business. Most important, it generates support for you and your initiatives. That support is so crucial on the road to success that it is worth protecting and defending.

Unfortunately, though, sometimes things go awry, or a person goes awry, and the values that underlie the organization, project, or relationship are violated. The next chapter explains what to do when this happens to make sure that your good reputation endures all the ups and downs.

NOTES

1. Remarks by Chairman Alan Greenspan, published by The Federal Reserve Board. Accessed at www.federalreserve.gov/boarddocs/speeches/1999/199906102.htm.

2. David Hakala, "The top 10 leadership qualities," *HR World*, www.hrworld.com/features/top-10-leadership-qualities-031908, March 19, 2008.

chapter 11

Overcoming
Threats to Trust

When you work, you bring your whole self with you. It is important that you are trusted and, with that understanding, you also have to recognize that your personal values must mirror your organization and vice versa.

People trust you if you are genuine.

—Alberto Ibarguen, president and chief executive
of the John S. and James L. Knight Foundation

I REMEMBER A neighbor of mine who worked at a company that manufactured and sold household products. The company had a reputation for being fiercely competitive, not only in the marketplace but also within its management ranks by encouraging a "survival of the ruthless" kind of culture. There was a legendary war room where executives would meet and take turns reporting on quarterly performance for their particular line of products. This exercise was likened to "shooting fish in a barrel."

My neighbor had done well at the company for a time and then lost out to those more manipulative than he. He gave me fair warning based on his experience. "Be careful," he said, "when you are going up the ladder of success, not to step on another's hand because it might be your hand one day as you are coming down while another is climbing up."

A Scramble for Power

Along with workplace dynamics that are positive and constructive to building reputations, there are, unfortunately, also negative forces at work. Chief among them is office politics, which can be found in virtually every company or institution.

It seems that when people come together in an organizational environment—where there is competition for roles, status, or rewards—an irresistible force overcomes them and they behave in ways that allow the ego to ride roughshod over getting the job done. The team can become subordinate to the individual . . . and you can get caught up in the scramble for power.

Office politics can take many forms, from the petty to the career altering. When you put a group of people together—each with his or her own ambitions, styles, values, morals, and backgrounds—you likely will have conflict. Some of that conflict is healthy because it fosters new thinking and pushes boundaries. But some of it can be destructive.

There can be jealousy over the symbols of power—such as work space, furniture, parking, access to the newest and latest technology, digital gadgets, touch pads, smartphones, and electronic devices. And there can be other concerns over titles, salaries, work assignments, promotions, and new assignments. The former are more easily addressed. The latter can sometimes run deep and foster behavior that undermines any organization, small or large.

For some, too often, there just doesn't seem to be an easy way to escape.

The concern is that office politics can quickly undermine a culture of trust. When it strikes, you become reluctant to trust others. In short, you question intent. You wonder what their motive really is and, in turn, you distrust their behavior. You sense that it is disingenuous.

Unfortunately, office politics do tend to be mean and even ruthless. Most often a person engaged in it has a hidden agenda. You may not know all the details but your instinct tells you not to trust that individual. You don't believe that the other's agenda and behavior warrants your trust.

A Short-Lived Advantage

However it is described, for those most skilled and manipulative, office politics can seem at first to help a career. Some can advance to more senior roles unusually quickly or without what would otherwise be the required qualifications. They might leapfrog the rest. On the surface, it might look like a traditional promotion or new opportunity, but, when examined more closely, there are questions.

Soon enough, some want to understand more clearly why the promotion was made. And, since others likely know the individual whose advancement has been questioned, doubts surface. Somehow, it just doesn't fit.

A cancer of sorts has started to grow. Motives are suspect. The answers are not forthcoming. And a feeling that things are unfair starts to surface.

While politics and political maneuvering may be better accepted in some quarters, among those working hard to create successful business careers they can be divisive. Individuals feel the stress because doubts have been created and the organization bears the brunt of the distraction. Talk turns to politics and time is wasted chatting in the halls, gossiping online, and sending texts. Internal politics becomes divisive. It hampers getting the work done, selling products and services, hiring new people, and handling other essential tasks.

In these kinds of situations, any seeming early success could well be short-lived since there, undoubtedly, will be someone within the organization who will uncover the otherwise hidden agenda. If that doesn't happen soon enough, there will be someone even more ruthless and better at politicking who will do the person in at some point down the road.

When it comes to politics, jealousy rules the day. The fact is that there is always someone determined to take the time to outdo a colleague. Questions are raised. The more devious will start rumors to undermine the decision. There will be backstabbing in the office and on social networking sites. Talking about others becomes commonplace and saps valuable energy.

The reaction within the organization can take many forms. It can range from isolation of the individual who seems to have benefited from office politics to paying too much attention to him or her because that person is seen as a "favorite" and therefore presumed to wield power. Some will avoid any involvement, while others will lobby for their own benefit.

Regardless, the environment turns sour and people may become angry, hurt, irritated, or just plain fed up with a business environment in which politics plays such a seemingly important role. Those who are angry act out their anger in the workplace. Those who are hurt sidetrack themselves from the day-to-day and from their work. Those who are irritated grumble, complain, and generally lose the focus they need to do a great job. And those who are fed up put their resumes on the street and prepare to walk away to a new job.

If you find this kind of rough-and-tough "office politics" environment unacceptable, you probably have little choice but to look elsewhere for a new job. The facts are that it's unlikely to change any time soon, you probably wouldn't do well over the long haul, and your career will be short-lived.

Rising Above the Politics

Stephen M. R. Covey, author of *The Speed of Trust: The One Thing That Changes Everything*, in his book delved deeply into the concept of "intent" and the role it plays in generating trust. He zeroed in on trust as a key element of effective management. He looked closely at the intentions of a manager and the kind of impact those intentions have on a manager's ability to be trusted. He looked at an individual's intentions, believing that they play a critical role in understanding motive and agenda—hidden or in plain sight—and, obviously, the behavior that followed.

By urging that intent, motive, agenda, and behavior must be aligned, Covey not only outlines a path for effective management but also sends up a warning flag on office politics. When there is alignment, he believes, the four—intent, motive, agenda, and behavior—work together in a way that generates trust and creates a constructive and supportive work environment.

I would add another element to Covey's thinking: while the individual's intent, motive, agenda, and behavior must be aligned, so must there be alignment with the culture and values of the organization. The individual and the organization must be in sync.

Without that common purpose, behavior, goals, and values, office politics can run rampant and management's effectiveness will be diminished. When aligned, though, leadership and the entire organization can turn its attention to those actions that are productive and lead to success rather than those that are destructive and distracting and, as a result, keep people from working their hardest and helping the organization grow.

So what do you do about office politics? Simply put, you have to make sure your intent is transparent, your motives are clear, and your behavior is always in keeping with your values. Above all, you need all elements of your behavior to be in keeping with your reputation . . . even when the pressure to do otherwise may be great.

When confronted with a highly political environment, here are some principles to keep in mind:

- *Be clear and straightforward.* Take the time to be open and ensure that those with whom you work hear and know your motives and understand your principles.

- *Understand your own motives.* Have a clear picture of why you do what you do. Make sure those around you have the same picture.

- *Don't play the game.* Do your best to stay above the fray and above politics. In the long run, your credibility will benefit.

- *Keep your dignity.* Don't gossip. Don't do the very things that you dislike.

- *Focus on the job.* You can't help but listen to what is going on, but don't let that be your focus. Keep doing what you do best and, with time, you will emerge the better for it.

- *Be smart.* Don't be naive. You shouldn't play the game but then again, you shouldn't ignore it either. Pay attention so that you are aware of what is going on.

- *Plan your career.* Look for new assignments that give you a chance to demonstrate your talent. Keep your eye on a career track, not a political one.

- *Don't overreact.* If you are the subject of gossip and attacks, respond only in a reasoned way. Don't get emotional. Look at things in an objective manner.

- *But don't roll over.* If you are attacked, have your facts and figures ready. If necessary, look for ways to demonstrate your values and performance. Keep it factual.

If those principles don't work for you, look for another position. The current one clearly won't work for you in the long run. It is time to leave. But be smart in finding that new job.

Is this easier said than done? Of course. But it might actually be the simplest and best path in the long run because you will avoid wasting valuable years pursuing a career in an organization where you cannot and will not thrive. Those career detours can be costly from every perspective—for your reputation and otherwise.

You must ultimately decide for yourself how best to handle office politics. Whether we like it or not, its existence is a harsh fact of life.

Take a Stand

What if you decide that someone needs to leave the organization because his or her actions undermine trust or are detrimental to reputation?

In his characteristically direct style, John Maltese, a retired chief financial officer, put it this way:

> Unfortunately, some apples weren't good. When I found a bad one, I had no choice but to extract it, as not to ruin the others, or for that matter, so as not to ruin what had become "our" reputation . . . the reputation of the team that I managed. This was probably the most difficult part of my job but it was essential.

Experience will support John's view. In fact, most successful businesspeople will tell you that, when they had to punish or make changes, they wish they had done more and done it sooner than they did.

Sticking your head in the sand to delay or avoid tough decisions never is a good approach. Ostriches aren't my favorite animal. My pilot training prepared me for the worst and never to shy away from addressing potential problems, even if none had yet surfaced. My view was that we always had to be ready simply because it is dangerous if possibly troublesome and sensitive issues go without open discussion.

I asked myself, If trust is so important to reputation, shouldn't we purposely review some of the situations and responses that might undermine or destroy trust? Shouldn't we try to think through how we would behave if something went wrong?

My answer was simple: Yes.

To me, those discussions were "mental rehearsals" to try to anticipate a problem and look for solutions in advance. Their goal was to talk about "what if."

With that in mind, I started to raise trust issues. When I held a leadership meeting or dinner in the United States or in another part of the world, I would pose a hypothetical question surrounding, for example, what the team members would do if they discovered someone had done something improper with the financial reporting. Or, in another example, we would talk through what would be management's actions if someone otherwise behaved inappropriately. At first, the response to these discussions was one of curiosity . . . with a tinge of offense. Those who seemed offended thought I was accusing them of something. But that was far from the truth.

The real point to my questions was to ensure that everyone understood that these kinds of topics were important and should be put on the table for discussion. Whether we like it or not, sometimes, somewhere, someone will do something wrong. That is a given. The important question is, How do we respond?

My view was direct and straightforward. If trust was a value that was crucial to our success, then we had to talk about it, both what we do to ensure trust and what we would do if it were breached.

As unexpected as these discussions were at first, a stake was put in the ground. With time, those open discussions took hold and became a healthy forum for looking at our values and, therefore, our reputation.

Anticipating Threats

With time, we want to have anticipated situations that could be challenging or those that could threaten our business enterprise. If we didn't, we might lose control, possibly jeopardizing our ability to make the tough decisions needed when it comes to values and reputation. Because they're unexpected—because we didn't anticipate them—we might not have the time or opportunity to clearly think through such situations, and might not keep in mind the importance of the values and insights that should underlie our decisions.

So what are the warning signals of a possible threat?
From individuals:

❙ Behavior changes.

❙ Work performance drops off.

❙ Conflicts with colleagues emerge.

❙ Rumors circulate.

❙ Individuals are asked off teams or not selected for assignments.

❙ Work and family balance is lost.

❙ Personal problems enter the workplace.

❙ An increased number of employee resumes are "on the street."

From the company itself:

❙ Sales drop off.

❙ Rumors circulate about financial or other problems.

❙ Management behavior changes.

❙ Communications are stifled.

❙ Information is withheld.

❙ You start hearing disturbing stories about the organization from outside.

From the perspective of both the individual and the organization, one of the most challenging and disturbing issues to face is a growing concern that an employee has done something improper, violating a core value or violating the law. As difficult as that might be to accept, it happens more often than we wish.

You have to keep your antennae up. As the old adage goes, *Where there's smoke, there's fire.* And, if you miss the signals, you have no one to blame but yourself.

The guideline is that, if you think there might be a problem, there probably is. Stop, look, and listen. Walk the halls. Listen to what people say and how they say it. Use your discretion. Network to learn what others outside the organization are saying. And don't ignore the signals of a looming problem.

Those same concerns are the ones that threaten your personal and professional reputation, and could threaten the values, integrity, and reputation of your organization.

The Need for Consequences

You need always remember that shaping and managing your reputation is a never-ending process. You will face dramatically different kinds of situations at various stages in your life and your career. Each one of them will test your convictions: your ability to remain true to your values when pressures mount. And they will mount.

Consequences and punishments for behavior that is unacceptable are very powerful statements. Defending values is a key element of your reputation. It speaks to your values and your strength. Moreover, how you behave in situations that test and challenge your values provides others with clear evidence as to whether you have the strength and determination to enforce the kind of behavior that is crucial for both your and the organization's long-term success.

Steve Joenk, president and CEO of AXA Equitable Funds Management Group, LLC, shares what he sees as the importance of taking a firm stand.

> I have learned to take the long-term view. Sometimes there are challenges and you will have to take a stand. It might not be popular with some of those you work with or for. But, what matters most is that you did what you thought was right, took a stand, and, when you go home at night, you can look at yourself in the mirror and feel comfortable with what you see.
>
> I am an eternal optimist and believe that what is right will prevail as long as we remain true to our beliefs.

Consequences are critical. There can be no strength, conviction, or genuine reputation without accepting consequences and without being able to call for their delivery, or to deliver them yourself.

If someone has violated one of the principles or values that are at the cornerstone of your organization and therefore endangers your own reputation, you need to act. Sometimes, the situation is clear-cut. For example, if someone steals, treats another in a manner that violates his or her rights, or commits some other kind of crime, the violation is undisputed. Chances are, that person will need to be terminated from his or her position.

But what if the situation is not so clear-cut? What if there are no facts, or the facts that emerge are not definitive? What if there are conflicting opinions as to what happened? When do you have to take a stand? The choice is yours, but there are no definitive answers. Your experience and best judgment must prevail.

Punishment with Fairness

When punishment is warranted, what are some of the choices?

The range of punishments varies. From mildest to most severe, they include:

▌Private conversation

▌Warning

▌Stern rebuke

▌Demand for an apology

▌Demotion

▌Loss of a bonus payment

▌Loss of a stock/share award

▌Forced resignation

▌Termination

▌Termination for cause

If an employee has violated basic principles, someone may well need to say something to the rest of the people who work at the company, or even make a public statement about the situation. Taking this step is very serious, and a decision made only with a full understanding of what has transpired. Beforehand, of course, there must be a thorough investigation so the company has all the facts.

This entire process must be fair. If the company has done its best to investigate in an objective manner and finds that the behavior violates an important principle, public exposure and punishment can well be the next step. That kind of action can underscore your reputation, not only because you demand the best behavior from the people you work with but also because you also have the courage of your convictions to enforce the rules when standards are violated.

A public display of consequences can be very powerful indeed. And that may be essential. The sad fact is that people sometimes need to see consequences and punishment—both of which must be warranted—before they will take values seriously. They need to see things in action before they believe they are real.

Enforce Your Standards

Taking this step is no different from any form of enforcement. Violations demand it. Your mettle is tested. Enforcing your standards is key. It is felt not only by those in your organization but also by those with whom you do business or partner strategically or use as suppliers. They too watch and talk about what you do and how you do it. The effect on them is both positive and a warning. It is positive because it is a clear demonstration that you behave in accord with your values and enforce what you hold dear. It is a warning because it sends a strong signal letting them know that if they don't adhere to the same values and have the same level of integrity you do, their prized relationship with you may be terminated. Either way, enforcement fosters a stronger sense of trust and clarifies the expectations. Your reputation for fairness strengthens.

The corollary is also true. If you fail to enforce or call attention to problems, few will follow you or trust you in the future. Like children, they will quickly learn that your rules are made to be broken and, when broken, there are no consequences. As a result, trust is destroyed and reputations are lost.

As time goes by and we face career challenges, the way we handle each of them gives us the opportunity to learn more about ourselves and about what ultimately matters most. This makes us able to think more clearly and objectively.

But what do you do when the situation is the result of your own decision or action? Something important has gone wrong. Do you shoulder the responsibility and accept the consequences, or do you try to find a way out? We are all human; we all make mistakes.

The next chapter provides advice about what to do when that happens.

chapter 12

When You Make a Mistake

It is okay to make mistakes because your reputation is made by how you handle those mistakes. After all, we do make mistakes. What happens after the mistake is what counts and what's most important.

—Steve Joenk, president and CEO of AXA
Equitable Funds Management Group, LLC

FEW THINGS STRIKE fear in the hearts of anyone as quickly and as dramatically as realizing they have made a big mistake.

While we all make mistakes in our jobs, we generally do not spend too much time worrying about whether those could derail our career or damage our reputation, or the reputation of our organization. We take responsibility, pick up the pieces, correct any problems that may have resulted, and move forward. In truth, we know this is what we have to do as managers because part of our job is to make decisions and lead, and in that there is always risk. We are fully aware that we are judged by our successes, our ability to solve problems, and our willingness to correct mistakes.

Mistakes, unfortunately, are simply a fact of life. We all make them and have to deal with them. *We are only human,* as the saying goes.

Big mistakes are different, though. They come with fear. They have a way of jolting our sense of security and even our confidence, much like being startled out of a deep sleep, sitting up, and finding that the nightmare is not imagined but is rather very real.

We face this kind of fear and trepidation when important decisions go wrong; for example, when our strategy did not deliver, the hard-fought investment missed the forecast return, or the dramatic change we made in the leadership roles took far too long to take hold and the organization lost crucial ground to competitors. These are but a few of the kinds of major operational, financial, or strategic decisions that have an impact on, and significant consequences for, success and reputation.

When you consider all the decisions you are called upon to make in your career, you can be sure there will be at least one time when a situation takes a serious and unexpected turn for the worse. Perhaps you were not able to carve out enough time to perform all the necessary research, weigh the various options, or consider all likely outcomes. Or you might have been confident that you were on the right track and had logically followed through as planned. However, regardless of the circumstances, the decision you made turned out to be wrong.

Perhaps the mistake resulted not from the decision you made but from circumstances that could never have been predicted. We know there is always the chance of a wild card. Regardless of how well we plan, how much time we invest in preparation and research, and how much input we receive from others, something somehow can always go wrong. The unexpected happens. It seems almost inevitable.

Quite possibly, the root of the problem might have started to grow before you even joined the organization. You might be relatively new to your role in the company and have inherited a problem sown by your predecessor. In spite of your best intentions and most thorough review, a crisis erupted and—regardless of who is responsible for its origin—it now rests in your lap because it occurred on your watch.

When a mistake is made, the fact that something went awry is not the only issue. There is no doubt that mistakes are a setback. When they occur, we lose time and resources—financial and otherwise—and have to go back to the drawing board. Moreover, mistakes can damage reputations…both yours and the organization's.

Resources are finite and should not be wasted, regardless of where we work. If we are managers of a business, the owners and shareholders have an eye on reputation, market share, and the bottom line. If we are part of a nonprofit organization, an educational institution, or a medical facility, we have a responsibility to those who fund our operations to make effective use of donations and other private or public monies.

We also need to remember that doing something twice is always more costly than doing it right the first time. And having to do something three times is tough to forgive. Just as in baseball, three strikes and you are out.

A Two-Part Analysis for Recovery

Most of the time, we have the opportunity to address a mistake, find another solution, make a correction, and give it another try. We are also in a unique position to achieve a longer-term goal: to make sure similar mistakes do not happen again. We need to take a candid look back at how the mistake happened and perform a two-part analysis: factual and personal.

The factual, or practical, analysis requires us to understand the facts and take what some call a "deep dive" to examine the circumstances that led up to the mistake. Straightforward answers to some tough operational and management questions are the start. We start that process by collecting facts and digging as deeply as possible to make sure that there is nothing we have missed.

The format for doing that from inside the business is to call on one or more of the following:

I Finance

I Operations

I Audit

I Legal

You also might consider putting together a small team of respected managers who are vested with the authority to gather information and prepare an analysis.

Sometimes, however, you need to bring in outside experts who, because of their objectivity, will likely ask a broader range of questions and perhaps more probing ones. For example, those experts could be:

▌Independent legal counsel

▌Management consultants

▌Strategic or operational advisers

▌Investigative and security firms

▌Accountants and CPAs

Is there an expense to this "deep dive"? Yes, whichever means of analysis you choose. There is a resource and financial expense in terms of lost man-hours whether internal people need to be assigned this task or hard dollars need to be spent for outside experts.

Regardless, completing this kind of factual analysis is only the beginning and, in most cases, it is also the easiest part of the review.

Far more difficult is your personal analysis. You face a tremendous challenge and a serious test of your character in order to be objective when you and your career might be under attack.

The important questions to ask yourself are:

▌What role did I play?

▌What was my responsibility?

▌What could I have done differently?

▌How am I now going to rectify the situation?

▌Am I going to take full responsibility and address the problem head-on?

▌Or will I try to behave as if the mistake is not really a problem or attempt to justify my decision from some other perspective?

The Road Back

Regardless of how we analyze the situation, when we make a mistake, it becomes very personal. Those around us develop their own opinions of our performance—and reputation. Many are quick to pass judgment and they often do so based on few details and sketchy information. They may also be influenced by comments they have heard from others or even the rumor mill.

The toughest challenge comes when we do so wish that the mistake was not our fault or did not happen, especially on our watch. The first impulse and temptation may be to deflect the criticism, find an excuse, or keep some distance from team members and critics alike. That is when it gets really tough.

These can be cruel moments and you cannot help but take it all personally. You may well feel unjustly treated. Nonetheless, you need to deal with the problem directly. The best way to do that is not to shy away or shirk responsibility.

What specifically should you do? Here are some important steps to follow:

I *Step back and take a deep breath.* Before you act, give yourself some breathing room and think. Take an objective look at the problem and how, what, and why it happened. Avoid acting prematurely and impulsively. Do not make a decision until you have as much factual information as you can gather and you have the benefit of all available input.

I *Resist the temptation to deny because cover-ups fail.* Time and time again, history has shown that those who deny a problem—or their involvement in it—or attempt a cover-up will fail. In the short run, walking away from a tough situation might get you another night of restful sleep, but in the long run the nightmare will return.

I *Put your ego aside.* Egos get in the way of wise decision making, especially when you believe you have been personally attacked or you are vulnerable to criticism. If your response is fueled by protecting your ego, chances are you will do the wrong thing. The worst step you can take is to overreact and put your interests first, with the goal of protecting yourself. That is the quickest route to losing your personal credibility.

❙ *Obtain advice.* Talk to experts who have experienced similar situations and listen to what they have to say. They are better able to be more objective than you could possibly be at this time, and their advice will be more reasoned.

❙ *Look to the future.* Focus not only on solving the problem and minimizing its fallout but also on avoiding its recurrence. After the analysis, are you putting checks and balances and other preventive measures in place to avoid a similar problem from happening in the future?

❙ *View yourself from different perspectives and vantage points.* Think of how others may be viewing you and your actions . . . and forming their opinions. Put yourself in their position. Do they trust you? Are you believable? Are your motives clear?

❙ *Be introspective.* Did you do something that may have caused the mistake? Is there anything that you should have done differently? After any mistake—after any crisis—there are always changes that need to be made.

❙ *Think seriously about an apology.* It could be the right thing to do. It could permit a fresh start. If you do apologize, though, be sure it is genuine. An apology that rings hollow is worse than no apology at all.

The Apology

For many, the three most difficult words to say are *I am sorry.* When spoken to express compassion for someone else's misfortune or in the aftermath of a tragedy, the words flow relatively easily. However, when they are used to apologize for having made a mistake, those words struggle to come out. For some, there are no other words that can make them feel more vulnerable. For others, the words can be humiliating.

Yet, *I am sorry* can also be disarming, candid, and full of character and maturity. It can foster a sense of understanding and forgiveness, and offer the possibility of a fresh start. The fact is that most people are willing to forgive and offer a new beginning if the individual has the honesty and integrity to accept responsibility for a mistake and apologize. This approach, which we so often follow in our private lives, applies just as strongly to our career and our public life.

So the question then becomes: *Do you or do you not apologize for a mistake?*

This is one of the toughest decisions you can make. In answering that question, you need to consider your values and the impact of an apology on your organization and on your reputation. Of course, whatever you decide, you must be sincere.

The business world is filled with instances of people who failed to apologize when others believed the situation warranted it. In fact, it is most egregious when those at fault fail to show any remorse or contrition for their mistake. Whatever the reason—ego, poor advice, or simply stubbornness—they abandoned the chance of support and lost the opportunity to rebuild their reputation by earning the forgiveness and trust of those who mattered. Ultimately, their own behavior did them in.

Moreover, a denial, if not solidly based in fact, will haunt you forever. As we all have seen, eventually the truth will emerge and the cover-up may well be worse than the mistake.

Likewise, beware of the empty apology. It becomes transparent very quickly.

What to Do—From the Experts

Earning support and, if necessary, rebuilding a reputation are day-to-day jobs that we need to take one step at a time, whether recognizing a mistake, correcting a problem, or moving forward to embrace success. This holds true for everyone, at all levels, in all types of organizations.

While one major mistake can deliver a severe blow, if handled properly it is not always fatal. Research findings support the belief of many reputation strategists, management consultants, communications professionals, and other experts that reputations can be rebuilt. They may debate over how long it will take, but they believe it can be done.

There are a number of action steps you can take that are focused on restoring and strengthening your reputation after a mistake is made, a crisis strikes, or another kind of problem occurs. Consider these:

I Acknowledge the mistake.

I Apologize.

I Communicate forthrightly.

I Take responsibility for the problem.

I Take responsibility for the solution.

I Demonstrate clear direction with specific actions.

I Commit yourself and your team to doing a better job in the future.

I Share what you have learned.

I Report back on progress.

Twelve Hours or Else

The Internet and social networking media—Twitter, Facebook, BlackBerry Messenger, blogs, text messages, and the rapidly expanding range of other social media—have changed the way reputations are built and destroyed. With enormous reach and power to shape the views of many, social media have put new pressures on careers. When it comes to criticism of your decisions and behavior, the online world of social media clearly is a ticking time clock.

We have seen nothing like this before. The speed with which reputations are damaged—if not destroyed—is incredible. Information is transmitted instantly, rumors escalate, and individuals and organizations are pressured to take action based not on the facts but merely on what they have heard from others, saw on YouTube, or read on the Internet.

If social media can lead to unrest around the globe, just think what can happen to your career if you are criticized online for doing something wrong or making a mistake.

Your reputation hangs in the balance. So does your career. If you are too slow in your response, what others hear and read take over. Perception becomes cast in stone as if it were reality, all without a fair hearing. And, of course, bad news, gossip, and criticism win the day. They travel at unheard-of speeds and to locations in every corner of the globe.

Sadly enough, an apology—when delivered too late—doesn't have the impact it could have had. Lost time means lost advantage. You will be swept out by the rip current of what others say, regardless of the facts or your view.

The rule of thumb is this:

First, you need seriously to consider a response if there is a crisis in which social media have voiced criticism of your values, your decisions, your integrity, and your reputation, thereby putting your career in jeopardy.

Second, if you do respond, you must respond within twelve hours or you will be burned.

Wait too long and social media will take over. Whatever facts you might like to share or whatever information you have that could put a balanced perspective on the situation will be of little avail. It is too difficult to chase the story when—in the world of digital technology where nano seconds count—it has had such a long head start.

So remember . . . you have twelve hours or less within which to take responsibility and say, *I am sorry.* And within that same time, you will have to commit to a fresh start, assuring those around you that nothing like what happened will happen again.

It's critically important that you recognize the world for what it is today and realize the speed and power of social media.

Don't take chances. Get in there quickly. Take control of your reputation. Don't let others do it for you.

The Lion's Den

The imagery of entering a lion's den has come to represent the courage to enter a place of danger and foreboding. It also represents doing what is right in spite of possible danger, thereby finding great victory.

This applies equally to the courage to recover from a mistake.

Deciding to voice the three words—*I am sorry*—can be daunting. Yet, when it comes to reputation, it may well be one of the best career decisions you can make.

At the heart of mastering a tough situation—one in which you might well have been wrong—lies a clear mandate: take responsibility and do not run away. It is really quite simple and not at all complicated. Think about values and character. Focus on reputation for the long run. Keep the future in sight.

The Leadership Opportunity

The ironic thing about having to deal with a mistake is that it actually gives you the chance to emerge even stronger.

It is a singular leadership opportunity.

If you have done the deep dive of a practical analysis, had the courage to test your resolve by being introspective about your personal behavior, set in motion critical steps and new strategies for change and the road back, and showed your strength of character by apologizing, then the moment of great leadership can be yours.

At that point, your actions certainly have set you apart. Your integrity and courage—the values you project—are of what leadership legends are made. While people never tell you everything, they do notice far more than you might otherwise believe. In the long run, they give the greatest credit to strength of character.

And as we have come to recognize, character is indeed the starting point for an even stronger and more valued reputation.

With that, though, it becomes clear that the full leadership opportunity extends well beyond your handling of the mistake itself. Now you have the chance to start new initiatives, any one of which could take your career or your organization in new directions or to new heights.

However, that is up to you . . . and only you.

Think about it. Ask yourself: Can I do something more to ensure that others don't make the same mistake as I did? After all, in all likelihood my mistake wasn't so unique. Others will be faced by similar choices. Do we need a stronger research or an online media capability so that we are better informed and in a more timely manner? How about our people training and talent evaluation procedures? Are they as relevant and up-to-date as they should be? Could we pioneer some industry initiatives to create a more effective dialog—deeper engagement—with those who buy our services and products? Or with those with whom we partner and collaborate to develop the newest and the best solutions? Could we reach out and lead when it comes to new ideas that better serve our customers, clients, the environment, and safer procedures?

The list could be endless.

The challenge is simply not to let things slip back to the way they were. A mistake shines a bright light on some sort of problem. Your first task is to acknowledge the problem, apologize, fix it, and ensure it won't happen again.

Then the challenge is to see what else can be done. Taking that step is the leadership opportunity.

Understanding what to do when there is a mistake is an important career strategy that contributes to the enduring reputation we seek.

chapter 18

An Enduring Reputation

I see reputation as "moving along concentric circles."

Each new job was another concentric circle and the pattern had to begin again. In an organization as large as MetLife, I couldn't rely on my last job to get me ahead. It was the current assignment and then the next one that were key. Each new management job was another challenge . . . I viewed it as starting from scratch and building my reputation once again.

—Ted Athanassiades, retired vice chairman and president of MetLife

ONE OF THE MOST challenging lessons for each of us is that managing our own career is up to each of us alone. No one will build our career for us. Just like anything else of importance, we have to take charge and commit to the long term.

It doesn't happen overnight. And we must work on it every day, day after day.

It started with your very first job. Perhaps you had a part-time job in high school, working during the evenings, the weekends, the holiday seasons, or for the summers. You applied for the job, received the offer, and the first day arrived. When you walked in the door it was unfamiliar, perhaps even a little frightening. It was a new experience. Whether or not you realized it at the time, it was not just your first job . . . it was a crucial first step to your career and your reputation. From that day on, you had to prove yourself. If you didn't pass muster, you might have lost the job or, just as final, you weren't asked back to work the next season.

With each new job, you took another step to build your career and your reputation . . . new work, new successes, and meeting new challenges.

Working hard, performing well at each stage, developing relationships, and looking for increasingly demanding work experiences are just some of the elements to building your career and an enduring reputation that will lead to success.

Claude Ritman, executive director of Coler-Goldwater Hospital in New York City, shares his views of a reputation built over time.

> You have to work at your reputation. It doesn't just happen. You prove your work ethic at each turn. You develop strong personal relationships, particularly in a city hospital system where the fact that people get to know you becomes critical when choices are being made. And you have to prove yourself with a track record that isn't a "one-shot wonder."

As we build our careers, we begin to realize that an important part of building our reputation is a focus on understanding how others see us. We start to think about the qualities we demonstrate and we look for opportunities to shape the way we are seen. If we are serious, we work harder, show greater resolve, adhere to strong values, focus on our character, become engaged communicators, never violate trust, and demonstrate at every turn that we are thoughtful and caring.

As the quote from Socrates at the opening of this book says, "The way to gain a good reputation is to endeavor to be what you desire to appear."

Ted Athanassiades knows this well. He had a very clear philosophy that formed the foundation of his reputation and his career path. He tells it this way:

> I was quick to develop a pattern in the way I did my jobs and I was deliberate in following that pattern, year after year.
>
> This meant that I had to be ready for each new assignment and put as much, if not more, energy and time into that new assignment as I did my last.

I was at MetLife my entire working career. I started out in a group of clerks, doing calculations as an actuarial student. I worked hard from the start and one of the senior team noticed me. Soon, I was made a manager and my perspective changed. At that point, I realized that, for me to continue to advance, I had to encourage others to do their best. It was no longer sufficient to focus on my own world but I had to reach out to others. That meant that I had to pay attention to both what I did and, increasingly important, how I did it.

I developed a strategy for how I would work and for how I would be seen by others. It had three parts: first, of course, I had to do good work; second, I had to be willing to take a chance and have the courage to show initiative and do "breakthrough" work; and third, I wanted to communicate differently with those I worked with.

Good work is just a given.

Breakthrough work is a challenge. I had to look at the big picture, take a different perspective, and be willing to convince others of the merit in new ideas. It didn't always work but, over time, I was seen as someone who didn't tread water but saw things differently than others.

And I tried to communicate with those I managed in the same way that I wanted others to communicate with me. That meant I had to listen to what I was being told and empower my team to carry out what became "our" plans.

It is your reputation—demonstrated by your prior accomplishments and followed by the expectation of your performance in a new role—that forms the basis for a promotion or a new job. When that promotion or new job is earned, those around you celebrate. It is your reputation that they celebrate.

They are proud to have you on their team. When they announce internally and externally that you are with them, they want others also to know. Your reputation is that valuable. They want others to be equally proud, if not impressed. They may send a note by e-mail, distribute an internal memo, issue a press release, or post your arrival on the organization's website. Very often, the announcement includes your photo and a few paragraphs that share some of your qualities, work experience, and expectations of what you will bring to the team.

This sense of pride gives you a head start. However, like each step you took to get to this point, at each stage of your career you need to focus on your reputation and how you are seen by others. It demands as much work and concentration along the way as it did at the outset of your career—with that very first job.

Self-Assessment for Success

To make the most of your career and earn the success you deserve—broaden your experience, hasten the career timetable, and move up the ladder—it is important to know yourself. The key is to be more proactive than most and very confident in your resolve.

Along the way, you need to be absolutely candid in asking and answering three critical groups of questions about yourself and your career.

First: Am I introspective? Can I look back and objectively analyze what I did and, more important, why I chose that particular course of action?

This first group of questions is tough to address, and realistic answers take maturity and determination.

Second: Did my decisions work? Did they get me where I wanted to go? If I look clearly at the decisions I made and the motives behind them, did they actually produce the results I wanted? If not, what did I do about it, and were there consequences? And, very importantly, did my actions enhance my reputation in the process?

This second group of questions requires objectivity and reflection, both of which are sometimes difficult for managers, especially if they don't want to be seen as having made a mistake.

Third: Am I up to the test? Did I have the courage to take on new and different challenges, especially those that might put my values to the test? In short, am I capable, as the saying goes, of "walking into the lion's den"? Am I really capable of tackling the toughest challenges?

This last group of questions puts you under pressure to explore how determined you really are.

All of these questions require a frank self-assessment. While this certainly may be challenging, self-evaluations with candid answers are a critical step to moving up the career ladder quickly. We must be sure of our resolve and ability to handle the toughest kinds of assignments, even those that might, on the surface, appear to threaten our careers if they don't work out the way we want.

Master the Basics

Bill Segal—entrepreneur, small-business owner, and real estate attorney in South Florida—puts his strategy for building an enduring reputation very succinctly:

> When it comes to reputation, be no less meticulous and careful than if you scuba dive in unfamiliar waters—"plan your dive and dive your plan."
>
> Be smart. Think long term. When you tell your client that you are going to do something, there is no excuse for not doing it. Anything less is unacceptable. If I represent a client in a transaction, it is nowhere nearly as potentially dangerous as a dive in an area where I have never been before but it is no less important to do what you said you would do.
>
> It's all about the long term. My reputation—like my father's before me and, hopefully, my children's after me—is everything. A commitment to do the right thing is just that... a commitment. It is not complicated. Tell your customer or your client what you are going to do and then just do it. There are no excuses.

The following six tips are basic to career development. They cannot and should not be overlooked when you are building a lasting reputation. Together, they form a foundation for success.

1. *Manage your career.* Don't expect anyone else to do it for you.

2. *Seek new skills.* Look to additional education and training to better equip you for a new assignment or the next stage of your career. Look for that tough project that will stretch your talents and test your drive and capabilities.

3. *Build a network.* Create relationships with people inside and outside the organization who can help you with career opportunities—they may learn of job openings and think of your skills.

4. *Foster work relationships with your supervisor and human resources professionals.* Talk with them about new assignments. Be seen by those in charge as someone who is eager, willing, and able to step up to different challenges.

5. *Work smart.* Don't miss the chance to prove to everyone that you are the best person for the job.

6. *Exceed expectations.* Do more than what was asked of you. Come in early. Work late. Go the extra mile. It will be noticed.

Initiatives to Master Your Future

If you have been courageous enough to tackle the challenge of self-assessment and are comfortable that you have the basics mastered, here are nine initiatives you might want to put into place:

❙ *Don't separate the personal from the professional.* Remember that reputation follows you every day. There is no difference between your personal and your professional reputation. There is no difference between your individual reputation and that of the organization where you work.

❙ *Ask critical character questions.* If facing a tough decision, ask yourself these questions: Is there a precedent in the organization or elsewhere? Do I agree with the way that same kind of decision was made in the past? What would I do if there were no precedent and why? If the sheet of paper were blank, how would I decide what was right? On what would I base my decision?

❙ *Raise the tough issues.* Be up-front and willing to address head-on the most difficult topics. If decisions require value judgments or touch on issues of trust and character, help put them on the table so that team members have the benefit of discussing them with you and knowing where your priorities lie.

❙ *Step out of the box.* Seek out an assignment that might be a stretch for you. Think about an assignment to another location, inside or outside the country, or in a different career direction that would move you away from your comfort zone. Choose something where there are unknowns, perhaps a different culture, where your views on what is right and what is wrong would be tested.

❙ *Conduct a mental rehearsal.* Role-play by putting yourself in hypothetical situations that challenge your integrity and ethics. Perform some soul searching on decisions that might pit your values against results. Morals versus money. How do you react in those kinds of situations?

❙ *Take pains to relate your decisions to the organization's underlying values.* Talk about decisions from the perspective of organizational values and reputation. View your decisions through the lens of trust and character and determine whether the decisions pass muster. Speak up and be counted on how important it is to remain true to the values that underlie the organization.

❙ *Ensure there are consequences.* When principles and values have been ignored or even violated, there must be consequences. If there is no punishment, then you as the manager have lost your muscle, and the strength of your own value system fails under scrutiny. Your reputation will suffer dramatically. You will be ignored and left powerless.

❙ *Do a mental review of your day or your week.* Run through the day in your mind. Ask yourself, What did I do and why? What did my actions say about my leadership and reputation—trust, character, and communication? Do I believe that I lived up to my responsibilities? Perform this same exercise periodically, at least once a month, to gauge your long-term progress.

❙ *Plan your tomorrows.* Think about what you can do tomorrow that will help to make you stand out . . . for all the right reasons.

Reputation Means Results

When some people think about what it takes to be successful, they may too quickly focus only on what often are referred to as measurable results. Those are the results that are most easily quantifiable. Some say they are "hard" results, implying that any others are "soft" and thereby have less value and are less important.

If you run a business, for example, measurable or hard results would often be financial—such as earnings, shareholder returns, profitability, and the bottom line—or they might be market share or industry ranking. If you run a charitable organization, they revolve around contributions and meeting fundraising targets. If you manage a trade association, they might be winning legislative or regulatory changes and moving the needle on public opinion.

Without a doubt, there can be no question that these are absolutely critical goals. The fact is that without them there is no long-term success. It would be naive to think otherwise. You cannot have a successful business without earnings that sustain it and permit investments for the future. You cannot do the important work of a charitable organization without the fundraising that creates the opportunity to undertake vital research or provide aid to the needy. You cannot have a trade association that is regularly funded by its members if it doesn't reach its targets.

While we work to reach those measurable results, taking stock of our reputation along the way becomes equally important. While your reputation too often goes without extensive formal surveys and research, its importance becomes immediately obvious when we see the decisions people around us make. They act based on your reputation. They trust, or they don't. They believe, or they don't. They think you have their best interests at heart, or they don't. And they believe you are listening, or they don't.

And, in turn, their actions—their decisions—create the basis on which those measurable results become reality.

Strong businesspeople know how to make this connection between reputation and results. They also know that reputation is what endures.

When others talk about you, they may talk about those measurable results . . . such as how much money you made for the organization or raised for projects, or how many initiatives you launched. But those comments will be brief and matter-of-fact. No one will dwell on them for very long or with any personal feeling or emotion. Rather, most of the time will be spent talking, and often with more passion, about the kind of person you are, the values you hold dear, the way you treat others, the respect you have for those on your team, and the efforts you made to encourage them to always do their best and make decisions based on the right values.

This is just human nature. And, when all is said and done, it is what lasts.

chapter 14

Reputation Paves the Way

Reputation is at the heart of what I do. If I communicate openly and clearly, if I hear what I am being told by those who every day take on the challenge of reaching out to provide to the vulnerable and the needy, and if I follow through, I can develop strong relationships that enable me to do my job well. Simply put, I can accomplish so much more.

—Joe Becker, manager of agency relations for
Catholic Charities of the Archdiocese of New York

REPUTATION IS VERY powerful and it is crucial to success, whether you are measured by the way people perceive you or by the results you reach. A strong reputation—built on character, communication, and trust—is the foundation for lasting success.

Your reputation is yours to forge. It is yours. It is very personal. And you can shape it. At times, that might take your every fiber and a determination to behave in keeping with the values you hold dear. Yet the fact is that your reputation is shaped by your behavior . . . not just your words. Everyone watches what you do.

Success demands strength of character. It also demands respect for others, who will then follow you into new areas because they believe in you.

Communicate often and more often. Capture every chance to engage others, hear what they say, listen to what will add value, and give credit where credit is due. That kind of engagement and dialog builds a common bond and ensures common understanding.

Trust is crucial. It is the foundation of your career relationships. People will listen to you and look to you . . . if you trust them and they trust you.

In short, the reputation that emerges is the foundation from which you build your own success.

As Joe Becker went on to say, "My reputation is everything."

Your Reputation Precedes You

By all accounts Henry Ford was a genius, not only because he was able to make his cars more affordable by installing the first moving assembly line and using interchangeable parts, but also because he had an instinct about the importance of reputation and how to build it.

It was Ford who is reputed to have said, "You can't build a reputation on what you are going to do."

He knew that people would buy his car if they trusted that it was reliable, believed in it as the new age of transportation, heard that it was produced by an innovator, and knew that they could buy one. For that to happen, he knew they had to see it, drive it, and hear what others thought.

As John Chamberlain, noted journalist and author of *The Enterprising Americans*, wrote:

> The Ford saga has been told many times and from many angles, with Henry Ford himself providing a neat, rational explanation for every major decision made by his company. [He] was a brilliantly intuitive man.[1]

Ford knew the power of reputation. He wanted everyone to know that his car was the first gasoline-powered car in the United States. He wanted everyone to know that they could buy his Model T relatively inexpensively and that it would be reliable. He wanted everyone to know that it was his automobile that would make it possible for Americans to travel across the country, connecting families and communities.

He knew exactly what he was doing and he knew that the reputation of the Model T—or any future Ford automobile—depended on demonstrating its value. Over time, reputation would build, the Ford brand would climb, and even more sales would follow.

He knew that it would be naive to believe that promises would build a strong reputation for quality. Only proof would suffice.

His reputation and success are the stuff of history books and business lessons. In just less than twenty years, he would sell roughly 15 million Model T cars, each exactly the same as the other.

The Power of It All

A strong reputation is not the only factor driving your success, but it certainly is one of the most important. In fact, it works in many ways to help you build a successful career.

If we look at some of the opportunities that a strong reputation creates, there are many. Among them, a good reputation:

❙ Opens doors.

❙ Gives you a head start.

❙ Builds relationships.

❙ Encourages dialog and engagement.

❙ Fosters support.

❙ Gives you the benefit of the doubt.

❙ Permits quicker recovery when something goes wrong.

❙ Gives you a second chance.

❙ Builds word of mouth.

❙ Encourages trust.

❙ Entices customers to take a first look…then a second, and a third.

❙ Makes the phone ring from potential clients.

❙ Narrows and even removes the competition.

❙ Ensures a warm welcome.

❙ Spreads friendship.

❙ Creates a network.

❙ Makes praise all that much more genuine.

❙ Makes criticism more palatable.

❙ Brings promotions faster.

❙ Helps foster a supportive culture.

❙ Permits an openness and candor.

❙ Supports teamwork.

❙ Creates partnerships.

❙ Ensures that the phone is answered.

❙ Makes the new job search easier.

❙ Fosters acceptance of your ideas.

❙ Encourages others to do the right thing.

❙ Underscores respect.

❙ Builds a climate of integrity.

❙ Supports values.

❙ Sets a high standard of behavior.

❙ Communicates character.

❙ Speaks of drive and determination.

❙ Describes your personal "brand."

❙ Arrives before you do.

❙ Paves the way.

❙ Creates positive reactions.

❙ Sets a barrier to improper behavior.

❙ Supports doing the right thing.

❙ Brings smiles.

❙ And drives success.

The Power of Reputation Is Yours

Strength of character comes from within. You can't fake it. You must, though, work to ensure that those around you know and understand the beliefs, values, and convictions that underlie what you hold dear and how you behave. After all, they will judge you not only by what you say but, more important, by what you do. Behavior is paramount. How you behave demonstrates your character.

You must communicate by words and actions those very beliefs and convictions that form your character. That communication is a dialog—a conversation—in which you listen and talk. It is built out of a respect for others. And it forms the basis for understanding and mutual respect.

Trust is at the heart of reputation. Trust in others is giving them the opportunity to do what is right. Trust that others have in you is what gives you the opportunity to lead and be successful.

In short, always remember—

Building a strong reputation is one of your most important jobs. Do it well. Time and time again.

NOTE

1. John R. Chamberlain, *The Enterprising Americans—A Business History of the United States* (New York: Harper, 1963), p. 205.

index